MINIMALISM & HYGGE

HOW TO DECLUTTER YOUR LIFE & THE DANISH ART OF A HAPPY AND COZY LIFE

EDISON MONTGOMERY

Copyright © 2021.

All Rights Reserved. This book or any portion thereof may not be reproduced or used in any manner whatsoever without the express written permission of the publisher except for the use of brief quotations in a book review.

CONTENTS

MINIMALISM

Introduction	5
1. Is minimalism right for you?	19
2. What Minimalism Isn't	25
3. Reasons To Love Minimalism	35
4. Exactly How To Find The Perfect Type Of Minimalism For You	48
5. What Is Simple Living?	57
6. Mindfulness	70
7. The Minimalist Mindset Shift	85
8. Why Highly Sensitive People Need Minimalism	96
9. Quotes To Motivate You To Declutter	107
10. Questions To Help You Declutter More Effectively	123
11. Steps To Declutter Your Home	135
12. Easy Things To Get Rid Of	142
13. Easy Practices To Maintain A Clutter-Free House	155
14. Benefit Of Simplifying And Decluttering	170
Afterword	179

HYGGE

ABSTRACT	183
Introduction To Hygge	185
1. The Basic Essentials Of Hygge	195
2. The Procedure Upon The Practice Of The Art Of Hygge	205

3. Practicing The Art Of Hygge At Your Workplace — 257
4. Making A Backyard Garden Through The Art Of Hygge — 274
5. Why Danish People Are Among The Happiest People — 280
6. Achieving Personal And Household Harmony Through The Hygge Lifestyle — 289
7. The Basic Understanding To Happiness — 321
8. Why You Should Not Live A Life Of Rush And Continuous Sets Of Anxious – Unhappy Lifestyle — 330
9. Increasing Opportunities And Energy At Your Own Pace And Time — 336
10. Effects Of Colors On Feelings — 341
11. Self-Care And Survival — 344
12. Conclusion — 353

Free extra content — 357
DISCLAIMER — 359

MINIMALISM

How to Declutter Your Life

By
Edison Montgomery

© Copyright 2021

All rights reserved.

This document is geared towards providing exact and reliable information with regard to the topic and issue covered. The publication is sold with the idea that the publisher is not required to render accounting, officially permitted, or otherwise qualified services. If advice is necessary, legal or professional, a practiced individual in the profession should be ordered.

From a Declaration of Principles which was accepted and approved equally by a Committee of the American Bar Association and a Committee of Publishers and Associations.

In no way is it legal to reproduce, duplicate, or transmit any part of this document in either electronic means or in printed format. Recording of this publication is strictly prohibited, and any storage of this document is not allowed unless with written permission from the publisher. All rights reserved.

The information provided herein is stated to be truthful and consistent, in that any liability, in terms of inattention or otherwise, by any usage or abuse of any policies, processes, or directions contained within is the single and utter responsibility of the recipient reader. Under no circumstances will any legal responsibility or blame be held against the publisher for any reparation, damages, or monetary loss due to the information herein, either directly or indirectly.

Respective authors own all copyrights not held by the publisher.

The information herein is offered for informational purposes solely and is universal as so. The presentation of the information is without a contract or any type of guarantee assurance.

The trademarks that are used are without any consent, and the publication of the trademark is without permission or backing by the trademark owner. All trademarks and brands within this book are for clarifying purposes only and are owned by the owners themselves, not affiliated with this document.

INTRODUCTION

Have you ever before wondered about the history of minimalism? Or ever did you want to know what minimalism means as a way of life? Chances are that you have actually heard about it even if you do not practice it yourself. There is a rich background to the practice of minimalism dating back thousands of years. However, it is mixed with an artistic movement, evolved into what is a typical way of life today.

Specifying Minimalism

Minimalism, in my analysis, is removing the unfavorable things in your life. Many minimalists on YouTube define it - as a way of life in which, you only keep those things that add happiness or value to your life.

The lower line is that we all have things that we need to remove. Whether it is material things like clothes, or simply mind-clutter-like unconfident thoughts, it is necessary to identify these things and reclaim control of your living space.

So, what is this minimalism thing? It is quite simple: to be a minimalist, you have to live with less than 100 things. You cannot have a house, an automobile, or a television. You cannot have a career. You have to stay in unique, hard-to-pronounce locations all over the world. You should begin a blog site. You cannot have children, and you should be a young white man from a blessed history.

Minimalism isn't about any of those things; however, it can help you achieve them. If you prefer to live with fewer products and properties, or not to have a television or a car, or take a journey all over the world, only after that, minimalism can offer a hand.

Minimalism is a concept that can help you find flexibility. Flexibility from the features of the consumer culture we've built our lives around-namely, Genuine liberty.

Today's issue seems to be the meaning of what we assign to our stuff: we tend to give too much meaning to our things, frequently abandoning our health, our partnerships, our passions, our individual development, and our need to add to ourselves. If these things are crucial to you, then that's wonderful. Minimalism merely permits you to make these decisions conscious and more deliberate.

Minimalism is a method. It's a technique, meaning that it takes practice, and you do it intentionally and consistently. It is to live and focus on life in a way that really feels authentic and holistic.

Since we believe that our environment substantially influences all other facets of our lives, minimalists place a focus on personal belongings. It turns out scientific research and study that is in agreement on that particular front.

All of our valuables call for something from people- our time, our focus, our energy. With minimalism, we are exercising being willful with the important things we allow to take from us. And we're exercising recognition of the items we have, and only how they influence us: not so much quantity, yet quality.

The mantra has a tendency to be "less is more,"

However less of what? The 'what' is only as important as having fewer things. You want to hang on to the important things that make you truly feel complete and highlight your most genuine self. You declutter (or get rid of) the bulk of what's left. It challenges your mind and lifestyle like a healthy and balanced diet regimen and works out your body.

It's a way of thinking change.

Minimalism is a change of attitude, much like any other area of focused improvement. When you choose to be healthy and balanced, it requires you to change your mind-frame of food and exercise. As minimalism has a solid focus on prioritization, it heads towards other areas of your life. So, although you may start by decluttering your house, you end up improving your timetable and prioritizing your partnerships at both ends. Your mind begins to filter things differently from a built method.

The background of Minimalism

If you're searching for the far-off origins of minimalism, you can discover the elements throughout history. It offers you an idea of exactly how the principles of decreasing valuables enjoyed more importance to gain back then.

Now, if you seek an official dictionary interpretation of minimalism, it is likely that you won't find what you're searching for. That's because until very recently, the word minimalism wasn't used to define a lifestyle. In fact, it initially had absolutely nothing to do with clutter or personal belongings.

The term minimalism became preferred in the 50's and 60's as a popular trend first in music and after that, in art and design. The suggestions coincided- to get rid of the instrument or layout pieces of focus.

As minimalism came to be popular in house planning and design- those whitewashed images with a single element of focus- individuals, started observing the aesthetically attractive aspects of minimalism on their own. But that was only the start.

Minimalism is an activity toward simplicity and away from consumerism. You know the drill. Chances are, you have actually lived it. Both moms and dads functioning full-time-plus hours, often with a little problem from companies that have a bottom line. Welcome to a minimalist society.

This isn't a small-scale concern; it's something that's been a reality considering the Industrial

Change. That's when we refined from handcrafted products to devices and started production on a massive scale. Mass-production led to overproducing, which compelled us to find methods to make individuals purchase each of these added crap we generated.

Advertisements are targeted at making you motivated to desire something; and, obviously, when one company gets richer doing it, it ends up being the new criterion. Thus, usage, and waste, came to be a way of living, for social status more often than utility or needs.

It sounds like a mouthful; however, generally, people are pertaining to understand that even more stuff cannot bring happiness. It can only bring tension and duty even more.

One driver to this entire procedure has actually been the crazy advancement of the web. Do not get me wrong; I looove the internet. The bulk of the international populace is on the internet and the approaches for marketing without limits are significantly even more budget-friendly than television commercials and paper listings.

Now the advertisements are 'clever;' they are hyper-focused so that, you're only shown the things that you're likely to acquire or have purchased in the past. At the very least, these hyper-focused ads are showing what you were already interested in rather than encourage you to become interested in something you're not yet.

What is minimalism expected to do around consumerist criteria on the home front?

The result of consumerist culture has actually been really felt by the daily functioning course, particularly the post-recession. Both parents are functioning and the expense of living has continued to rise. The housing market collapsed, unemployment escalated, and many individuals ended up not being able to attain the material things- like houses- that used to be a priority before.

Discovering creative ways not to need a lot helped a logical trend to minimalism. Requiring fewer means, not killing yourself at a work you hate, it means not needing to ride the 'use and dump' wave.

Also, overconsumption isn't only for the well-off. No financial class is immune to the shiny brand - new gadget or plaything phenomenon. The only difference is the expense of the item itself.

Something provides us joy for a duration of time

and then stops. We desire to fill that delight gap with something brand-new.

The result is huge debt and a home jumbled with unused items that no longer offer a feeling of pleasure or purpose.

What is minimalism expected to do regarding these problems? Well, for one, you have a tendency to have more money with less clutter. However, more importantly, it offers us a remedy for this treadmill. It alters the game by changing our expectations. When you need less, you're not pressed to stay up to date with the purchasing trends. Working on your own to death doesn't appear so necessary. Thankfully, adapting to coping with 'fewer demands' doesn't seem so difficult any longer.

TYPES OF MINIMALIST

Many outside the culture presume that accepting Minimalism will certainly leave them feeling empty, deprived, and lonesome. However, ask a Minimalist and you will hear the opposite. With the help of my Minimalist buddies, I thought it would certainly be fun to create a list of some of the "kinds" of minimalists.

The Counter

The certain variety of the number of things they have matter to these Minimalists. Usually, a more logic-inclined individual generally, these Minimalists value numbers, discipline, and self-sacrifice. They delight in extremes.

The Novice

The beginner sees the advantages of Minimalism- the charm, the happiness, the flexibility the society enables him. Yet, it is still passing a hard time to get the ball rolling on their individual journey.

The Joy Seeker

Usually, the Joy Seeker is a Minimalist inspired by Marie Kondo's ideal vendor, "The Life-Altering Magic of Cleaning." The number of items these individuals have is not important to them, yet instead, it is more crucial that they are meticulously culturing and curating a house that surrounds them with only products that make them satisfied. These Minimalists might prefer to be labeled as Intentionalists.

The Intentionalist

Intentionalists are people concerned with awareness of the information of their daily lives. These individuals usually do not desire to be wasteful with their time, nor to bother themselves with clutter that exists without purpose.

The Huge Picture

The Huge Picture Minimalists look like ecologists, pet enthusiasts, or activists, in a way. They are typically Minimalists by default as opposed to intent because of their adherence to a stringent set of values in their everyday lives. Like a vegan may decide to drive a hybrid or fuel-conserving car, they are conscious of profligacy and recycling.

And they will choose to purchase products at a greater expense to ensure that, it is a moral selection that results in the very best for all associated with the purchase. They concern themselves with the workers, the pets that might be involved, or the effect on the atmosphere. They prefer to have less and add more to the world with their time and via "ballot" with their bucks by intentionally choosing what to purchase.

Quality over Quantity

These individuals choose to have fewer products so that they can own much better items. In a world where several products are created as inexpensively and as quickly as possible, I like that concept. These individuals may likewise delight in sustaining local artisans and companies.

Keep It Clean

These people most likely do not take pleasure in the work that goes into cleaning; but, they do value staying in a neat and cool environment, so they have actually assessed their priorities. The finest suggestions I reviewed when I started in the direction of a Minimalistic life, applies to this grouping. There is no magic with products one can purchase to organize many things effectively.

The Nostalgic Minimalist

These individuals, whether young or a lot more advanced in age, cling to the timeless notion that the world was a better, and more gratifying place when things were slower and a little quieter.

The Mental Health Motivated Minimalist

I would definitely risk saying that, this grouping in one way or another, specifies all the Minimalists. Some recognize it beforehand and use their psychological requirements as an inspiration for an extra frugal lifestyle, while others start under various terms and only realize the health advantages after being immersed in Minimalism temporarily.

Regardless, all concur that Minimalism provides the much required and appreciated the psychological quality and balance for weary minds.

New Life

Maybe they've lost a lover, a close relative, or endured a similar life-changing event. In the same way, a female will dramatically change her hairstyle in such an instance, these people want to begin again and wipe the slate clean of the memories and the tension. These individuals are recreating themselves.

The Unchained Minimalist

These individuals appreciate being free to wander without the worry of duty. They may or may not really want a Minimalist life, but are required to live this way by their living arrangements.

Bullshit-Free Space

When they begin, these individuals do not know anything about Minimalism. They only understand that they are fed up, annoyed, and all set to change. De-cluttering is easy for this group since they have strong, angry inspiration. Though maintaining their living quarters might not be as easy for them as soon as space is gotten rid of and the motivation begins to wane. I would certainly motivate anyone in this category (cough- the Moms) to choose other similar people to construct inspiration and inspire each other along the trip. De-cluttering your room may bring you joy for a certain period in your life. However, changing the routines and way of your life can genuinely free you.

Influenced By a Hoarder

The name speaks for itself. These individuals have actually either suffered from living with a person experiencing a hoarding mental illness, or they have experienced the impacts of such a situation.

Aesthetics

There is also a genre of Aesthetic Minimalists. These individuals like the appearance of Minimalist design, furniture, and living. They find it lovely and might not embrace the psychological, digital, or relationship sides of Minimalism. In fact, they tend to enjoy the method the design aims to the eye.

Minimalists tend to be broad-minded people who are prepared to consider different perspectives, eager to discover something new, and ready to give up a little to get a lot in return. Get to understand a Minimalist, or I encourage you to discover the subject on your own. You may simply find a side to yourself you never knew existed.

1
IS MINIMALISM RIGHT FOR YOU?

The minimal lifestyle is a movement that looks to curtail your belongings to only the crucial ones because life can be enjoyed richer and fuller with the unnecessary possessions eliminated. It is a growing trend that includes more than only young, single, 20-somethings. Many households are accepting the way of life.

Also, an increasing number of people are being introduced to the lifestyle on a daily basis. Perhaps, it might be your very first introduction too.

Some individuals get anxious when they hear the term "minimal." For them, it invokes images of destitution, bare wall surfaces, and vacant cupboards. Appropriately so, they determine that it has no chance to be a delight in their life. Believe me, I concur- that is no way to enjoy life. And since choosing to end up being minimal, years ago, we have actually gotten on a journey to define what it means for us and how it fits into our unique lifestyle.

Well, first off, minimalism is not all about white walls and IKEA furniture that suits a 500 square foot area. While that can be minimalism to some, it's not for every person. Many individuals who live a minimal lifestyle may have brilliantly colored walls and huge comfy chairs, and every little thing in between. What's at the core of the minimalist movement is the idea of allowing and letting things go.

It's the idea that you need to organize the things in your home: to say YES to things that make you pleased and NO to the things that do not, or have gone way past their lifecycle. Is minimalism right for you?

To establish whether minimalism might be the ideal lifestyle for you undoubtedly, think about some of these questions:

1. Do you spend excessive time cleaning?

If you delight in clean spaces but not in cleaning, minimalism simply might be your response. The easiest means to minimize your cleaning time is to have fewer things. It functions every time.

2. Are you trying to get out of debt?

Financial obligation holds our life in bondage and weighs heavily on our shoulders. Getting a handle on it by purchasing fewer things is one of the best things you can do.

3. Too much stress and anxiety in your life?

Physical clutter results in additional tension in our lives. Minimalism gets rid of the mess and restricts the disturbance that it triggers. Minimalism may be the breath of fresh air that your house needs to help you loosen and liven up.

4. Would you like more time in your day?

Think for only a moment the amount of time that our belongings drain from our life. Whether we are cleaning, organizing, preserving, repairing, removing, or buying; our belongings need a large portion of our time. Owning fewer of them results in less time invested caring for them.

5. Are you eco mindful?

Minimalism reduces our effect on the environment by having fewer resources on the front end for manufacturing and decreasing the amount of waste on the backend. Nowadays, a new trend has been evolved. Eco-mindful individuals have started to believe in 'borrow-use-return' rather than 'take-make-waste'.

6. Are you prudent?

While becoming a minimalist does not imply that you need to invest less money, it absolutely provides the chance. Also, as you are getting fewer things, you have the alternative to make higher-quality acquisitions that last longer.

7. Do you delight in monetarily sustaining various other causes?

Minimalism gives an opportunity to not only save money for the sake of maintaining it, but also for using it to further your future possibilities. When you become content with your valuables and have been saved from the race of collecting possessions, you do not need to hoard money. You find new freedom to sustain the causes that you hold most dear. Lately, the Becoming Minimalist environment increased over $5,000 for Charity: Water.

8. Are there things you value more than material ownership?

Minimalism seeks to purposefully reveal things in life that we value the most and get rid of anything that sidetracks us from it. It permits us to focus on our deepest heart desires instead of the things for sale at the department store.

9. Are you unafraid of change?

Minimalism is a counter-cultural way of living that will certainly compel arrangements in the way you spend your energy, time, and money. Naturally, almost every change is good, so it values the effort to the fullest.

10. Is your life also useful to live like every person else?

Our hearts, spirit, and enthusiasms make us distinct and useful. Do not compromise your crucial role in this world by going for the same temporal belongings that everyone else in your environment is chasing after. Your life is much too important and brief.

Your certain method of minimalism is going to look different from anybody else. It must! Nevertheless, you live a various life than any other person. So find a design of minimalism that works for you. One that is not cumbersome, however releasing based on your values, needs, interests, and logical reasoning.

Eventually, you will begin to eliminate the unwanted things from your life. As a result, you will certainly discover space to intentionally advertise things you value the most and get rid of anything that sidetracks you from it.

2

WHAT MINIMALISM ISN'T

There is nobody single answer to the inquiry, "what is minimalism?" The idea of minimalism is really open to interpretation. As opposed to attempting to add every little thing that minimalism IS, it is a lot more practical to identify what minimalism is NOT.

There are a lot of typical misunderstandings regarding minimalism. Concepts that make minimalism seem harder to relate to it, unfavorable or out of reach for the typical individuals. By resolving these typical mistaken beliefs, I want to reveal to you that minimalism is achievable for and can profit anyone.

8 common mistaken beliefs about minimalism:

1. Minimalism has to do with eliminating every little thing you belong

It's true that a huge part of minimalism is removing things from your life. However, the focus of minimalism should not be on what you are doing away with. The emphasis must get on what you GAIN by releasing the important things that do not bring value to your life.

Rather than concentrating on what you're doing away with, focus on what minimalism offers you more of: even more time, even more room, even more peace, more liberty.

Minimalism is not about starvation. It has to do with deliberately choosing to deal with less in order to have even more time and room for what is most important in your life.

2. Minimalism is so limiting it makes life harder

A common mistaken belief is that minimalism makes life harder because you cope with so little.

That being a minimal way of doing away with everything but the bare fundamentals, consisting of things that make life easier.

A minimal life is much easier in numerous means. You invest less time cleaning, choosing, searching for things, maintaining your stuff, arranging your stuff, and so on. After taking on a minimalist way of thinking, many people see that things they believed made life less complicated and actually swiped their time and environment.

Minimalism is not about removing something if you actually use it frequently. In fact, It makes your life easier. It has to do with eliminating things that aren't used or needed and are simply cluttering your house.

3. Minimalism and economizing coincide with things

Thriftiness has to do with spending carefully and searching for chances to save money. A minimalist lifestyle can lead you to invest extra meticulously and conserve money, as you buy less and go shopping even more purposefully. However, being frugal is not always the primary intent of minimalism.

There are some overlaps between minimalism

and thriftiness, as both promote being deliberate of exactly how you invest your money. Some people might even turn towards minimalism in an initiative to be a lot thriftier.

However, minimalism and frugality are not the same. Minimalism goes beyond having less entirely for the function of saving money. Minimalism has to do with dealing with less in order to have the moment and room for what issues most in your life.

Additionally, minimalists might pick to buy fewer products but acquisition higher quality products. They are still deliberate about only how they invest by purchasing less. Yet are not focused on economizing because they are willing to invest more in the higher quality items.

4. If you are a minimalist, you cannot have pastimes or collections

A usual misunderstanding is that minimalism means you cannot help things you enjoy. Or you cannot have a collection that brings you delight. Or perhaps that you can't have a pastime that entails physical products.

Again, minimalism doesn't indicate you have to eliminate every little thing you belong to. Minimalism indicates being willful about what you keep — editing your ownerships to only the important things you make use of and like. Eliminating the excess enables you to use and take pleasure in things you love a lot more.

The key to minimalism is moderation. Rather than having 14 collections, decide to help 1 or 2 that you genuinely use or enjoy. It may indicate modifying your collection to only the best pieces so you can highlight those items and not shed them in a disordered collection.

If you have a leisure activity that needs physical materials, choose an environment to keep your products and be willful about closer alternatives. It's about deliberately curating what you maintain. Maintaining only the materials, you will actually use, rather than stockpiling products that are never used.

Minimalism is not about denying yourself the things you enjoy. The whole point of minimalism is to cut down all the excess so you can absolutely value, see and make use of the things you like.

5. Minimalism indicates stark, all-white rooms that look nasty and chilly

While there is a minimalist design aesthetic, typically identified by all-white rooms with little furnishings or décor, it doesn't mean to be the ONLY way minimalism can look.

Minimalism, as a way of living, doesn't have to look a specific way at all. Minimalism is when the only things you help in your location are those that you usually use and/or love. Minimalism is discovering the right amount of things for you.

What is enough will certainly be different for every person. The key is keeping only what adds value to your life and removing the rest. As long as every little thing in your space is something you either use commonly or absolutely enjoy-- that's minimalism!

Get particular about exactly how you desire minimalism to look and feel in your house. The term "comfortable minimalism" denotes a room that might be very little and clean but still relaxing.

It can help to use terms like this to get clear and particular about your vision of minimalism. Use this vision to create a minimalist house that benefits you. Don't fret about adhering to another person's visual.

6. You have to adhere to a specific collection of requirements or guidelines to be a real minimal

Some people do experiment with adhering to a specific collection of guidelines, like living with less than 100 things or having less than 37 items in their closet. But that is not the only method to be a minimalist.

The terrific aspect of minimalism is that you can produce your own collection of guidelines, and those rules can change as your life adornments.

Trying out with a collection of guidelines can be an intriguing and tough experience. Don't allow yourself to be turned off or limited by these guidelines.

Only bear in mind that minimalism is recognizing what you value most and getting rid of anything that doesn't line up with those values.

. . .

7. You cannot be a minimalist if you have kids. Minimalism only helps young, single people

Anyone can be minimal. It does not matter where you live or what you provide for work. It does not matter if you are single or have a big household.

I would say that the larger your family members, the more benefits you'll discover from minimalism. The more individuals in your house, the more things you tend to have. Getting rid of the excess and embracing a minimalist way of life can be even more important for households.

A minimalist who has a family will look different from a young, single minimalist. Neither is more or less minimal than the other.

In each instance, minimalism is about recognizing what they value most and removing the excess to make more room for what they value. Their values may differ. So, what they keep and do away with will certainly vary.

However, minimalism can benefit anyone or family, ready to put in the moment and effort to eliminate the extra in their lives and make room for what matters most.

. . .

8. Minimalism only applies to your things

Eliminating the excess stuff in your life is a huge component of minimalism first.

Yet "stuff" is really only one component of minimalism. In fact, a big component of embracing a minimalist lifestyle is moving your frame of mind about "things" completely. Learning to test and change your partnership with what you have and why you own it.

"I have actually found out that minimalism is not about what you have; it has to do with why you have it."

Minimalism really goes far past only what you own. It can be related to all areas of your life. Minimalism is all about identifying what you value the most in your life and removing anything that does not align with it.

The advantages of minimalism prolong all locations of your life, and minimalist suggestions can be used to lots of locations of your life other than simply your things.

Minimalism is a device, not the end objective. Minimalism isn't about possessing less for less.

Instead, minimalism is a tool that can help you

create the life you want and provide on your own the freedom to live that life. It's a device to help you live in a calculative way so that you can concentrate your time, space, energy, and focus on what issues most to you.

3
REASONS TO LOVE MINIMALISM

As somebody who writes about and strives to live a basic, minimalist life, it's not a surprise that I believe there are lots of reasons to like minimalism. Decluttering my home, simplifying my schedule and dedications, and changing my perspective about "stuff" have actually done wonders for my life.

The advantages of minimalism are the values the moment and initiatives

There are many things to love minimalism, some are small, some are life-changing. As I have actually said in the past, minimalism will look different for each of us, depending upon what we value and focus on. When you let and declutter the things you neither use nor desire, you begin to recognize the advantages of minimalism. The even more you release, the even more space you make in your life to experience these benefits.

At the beginning of your minimalism trip, it can be daunting and look like a lot of work. Completely upgrade your life, your house, and the means you live calls for persistence, time, and effort. But the outcomes of doing so are very much value it! There are numerous reasons to love minimalism. The advantages minimalism brings into your life are completely value the moment and effort it requires to get there.

Today I intend to share 15 reasons to like minimalism. To encourage, influence, and encourage you to place in the moment and effort to start experiencing the benefits of less!

1. More time and energy

Every single thing you have charges some of your time and energy. Some things deserve the moment and energy they need. Various other things aren't valued the quantity of time and energy they take up.

The even more things you have, the even more of your energy and time they use up. The less you have, the less energy and time you invest handling your "stuff," and the more energy and time you get to focus on your important belongings.

2. Even more environment

Normally, the fewer things you load your house with, the even more space you will certainly have in your home. With less stuff, you do not have storage rooms, and cellars jammed full. You have ample space since you do not have more than you need or use. You develop breathing space in your house when it has less mess and things.

In often, We assume that we need to build bigger houses, with bigger wardrobes and even more storage space. However, if you devote yourself to having less and only possessing things you use frequently or desire, you could not need as much room as you think, and you could understand you have ample room currently, you simply had excessive things!

3. Even more money

When you dedicate yourself to accepting minimalism and having less, you often tend to invest less money. only since choosing to have less means buying less.

A great side effect and reason to love minimalism is when you devote yourself to owning less and acquiring less, you also have a tendency to conserve money! Or possibly invest more money for things you really want to do, like travel.

4. less psychological clutter and even more focus

A cluttered house typically results in a cluttered mind. Your outside surrounding is commonly a reflection and mirror to your indoor state. When one is cluttered, disorderly, or in disarray, the other may tend to be additionally. You really feel overloaded, forgetful, or unable to concentrate because your environment contains mess and chaos.

You produce an even more soothing atmosphere when you reduce the clutter. Since there is less visual clutter and even more white space, an environment where your mind and eyes can rest. Your mind has an opportunity to come to be less messy and overwhelmed and you can focus much more conveniently.

5. Less anxiety

When your home is jumbled and chaotic, not only are you bombarded by visual clutter; however, your mind likewise needs to work so much harder. You need to bear in mind where things are amongst stacks of things. You shed things and ignore things, merely because there is too much stuff to keep an eye on.

Numerous means add stress to your life, also to shed your keys since they got shed under a heap of mess.

Owning less merely indicates you have fewer things, including stress in your life.

6. Much more liberty and adaptability

Another reason to love minimalism is that having less provides you so much more flexibility and flexibility. Not only will you have even more time, even more space, less anxiety, more money, etc.

The flexibility you acquire from minimalism looks different for all of us. Possibly it means you can have fun with your children much more and be the kind of mom and dad you want to be. Or perhaps it suggests you can work fewer hours since you don't spend as much money anymore. When you are unburdened and no longer evaluated down by so many things, perhaps you travel a lot more.

The freedom and versatility of minimalism give you variation from the little things to significant, life-changing things. However, the trick is minimalism, and owning less provides you the opportunities to develop the life you want. It frees up your money, room, and time so you can live your life the means you wish to. Rather than living the means, you need to because you're weighed down by stuff, commitments, and debt.

7. More time for things you like

You get more energy and time by having fewer things to care for. You have the chance to use that time and energy for what you really enjoy.

Possibly it's a leisure activity or task you intend to have even more energy and time for. Or maybe it's even more time and energy to invest with good friends or family members.

Whatever it is for you, owning fewer ways, you have more energy and time to commit to the things you love and make you delighted.

8. Enhanced connections

Continuing with that said though, minimalism offers you the possibility to boost your partnerships and focus more on the people you enjoy. Once again, when you have less stuff, you have more energy and time. This offers you the chance to concentrate on the family and friends that are most important to you.

It offers you the chance to play with your kids rather than simply tidying up regularly. Or to fulfill a close friend for coffee due to the fact that you have a lot more leisure time. Possibly it's more time to spend and connect with your partner instead of feeling drained and tired at the end of a long tiring day.

Minimalism additionally boosts your connections

by making you a lot more comfortable inviting people to your home. When you have less stuff, your home remains tidier with less initiative.

It looks for you, having even more time and energy to commit to the partnerships that matter most to you will certainly help those connections expand, prosper, and strengthen.

9. Cleansing is easier and faster

Having less means you have less to get, put away, tidy, arrange, etc. Generally, your house keeps cleaner and tidier since there is less stuff to make a mess with inside it.

The less you own, the faster and simpler the real cleaning jobs, like vacuuming, cleaning, wiping, and so on, become. Not only exist fewer products to tidy. Yet there is additionally less to obstruct while you're cleaning, so cleansing ends up being faster and simpler.

10. More eco-friendly

It leads us to purchase less when we pick to own

less. Every little thing we eat has an effect on the environment. Whatever air pollution is caused by manufacturing and shipping, all build up to the product packaging products. Having less and acquiring less lowers our ecological influence.

Likewise, when we devote ourselves to possessing less and purchasing less, we often tend to make more cautious acquiring choices. You start to value top quality over amount when you embrace minimalism. You typically investigate what you're getting, and try to find the best quality option. Much better quality items often tend to be less non-reusable and last much longer. Indicating there are less most likely to wind up in the landfill in only a brief time. Minimizing your environmental effect.

11. More clarity about that you are and what is very important to you

The whole point of minimalism is to determine what is crucial to you. Destroy anything that distracts you from it or does not line up with it.

Minimalism enables you to cut down unwanted belongings from your life so you have an opportunity to identify your values. And get a better understanding of your own identity. You discover what you value. and likewise, what you take pleasure in, what matters most to you and how you want to use your time and energy.

You might also use minimal ideologies to your schedule, aiming to simplify it and end up being less active. You begin to check out the commitments and tasks taking up your time. In addition, begin questioning if they add value to your life or otherwise. You end up being extra intentional with what you allow to take up both your time and your energy. Including both the physical things you possess, and the means you commit your time.

12. More self-self-confidence

It helps you become more self-positive. You gave up trying to "keep up with the Joneses," and recognize what you own doesn't determine your value.

The more you welcome it, the even more self-certain you come to be. Simply since you aren't gauging yourself well-valued by what you have, you tend to believe it as intrinsic. If you do not really feel good about yourself already, product ownership will certainly never make you feel good about yourself in the lengthy-term.

By breaking the connection between your viewed self-value and what you have, you offer on your own the possibility to get self-confidence.

13. Extra tranquil

When your space has less mess, you often tend to feel calmer and more relaxed.

Being bordered by turmoil and aesthetic mess makes it hard to loosen up, feel tranquil, and secure. A clutter-free, relaxed house makes it less complicated for you to feel extra kicked back and calm.

14. Less complicated to stay organized

The fewer things you have, the less time and effort you need to spend organizing. A lot more you accept and declutter minimalism, the less you also need to arrange at all.

When you have less, arranging comes to be a lot simpler, faster, and simpler to maintain. You don't need intricate business systems to find methods to fit as much stuff in an environment as feasible. You'll most likely have space to save.

Some company is always good so you have a place for every little thing you own and can find it quickly. The less you own, the less time and effort you need to spend organizing and keeping your organized spaces.

15. Much more appreciation

When you devote yourself to owning less, you become a lot more pleased with the things you have. Choosing to have less starts to cultivate a deep feeling of appreciation for what you have, as you end up being much more mindful of what enough looks like for you.

I was so focused on getting rid of stuff and not expecting to be happy, I remained conscious of what I kept. The effect minimalism has on feelings of satisfaction and gratitude is one of the precise reasons to enjoy minimalism for me.

We each have our reasons to love minimalism.

People are drawn to minimalism for their unique reasons. Yet generally, once we begin to accept minimalism, we recognize there are more reasons to enjoy minimalism.

Getting more time, more room, more flexibility are some other reasons to love minimalism. Accepting a life with fewer tensions allows you holistically experience the advantages of minimalism.

4
EXACTLY HOW TO FIND THE PERFECT TYPE OF MINIMALISM FOR YOU

I have already stated exactly how your type of minimalism will certainly be unique and personal to you. Your version of a straightforward minimal way of life won't necessarily match those of the others. But, it's more than okay! It's excellent.

Minimalism is not about following another person's guidelines or method of living as a minimal. Of course, your version of minimalism will certainly be unique to you!

There are no standards you need to follow to live an easy minimalist way of living.

It's wonderful that there are no strong guidelines to comply with to become a "key-minimal." Your life as a minimal doesn't have to match others. There is no examination to pass before you call yourself a minimalist.

Sometimes when you are only beginning on your

journey towards minimalism, it can feel frustrating to figure out how t. Occasionally you may seek a checklist of minimal "regulations" or minimal living pointers to follow to help you understand what you need to do to become a minimalist.

When I first began reducing and organizing, I know I was looking for some minimalist guidelines! I wanted to know the amount of each item I was "meant" to be minimal officially. It was hard not to contrast my type of minimalism with other individuals around me. I fretted that if I had two sets of sheets for each bed in our house, (I heard a well-known minimalist claim that, they only had one set of sheets,) that it implied I wasn't minimal enough.

At some point, I started recognizing that there are no minimalist policies. No one else can inform me what minimalism will certainly look like for my life and my family. My version of minimalism won't coincide with another person's type since all of us value different things. Most of us have different values, preferences, ways of livings, family dimensions, dynamics, and so on.

Although all our types of minimalism are unique to some extent, we can still call ourselves minimalists. The only "requirement" to be a "minimalist" is that you must recognize what matters to you and how you value it. Get rid of everything that isn't something valuable or important to you.

Undoubtedly, my version of minimalism is

special to me because what is vital and valuable to me is always one-of-a-kind to me.

Don't compare your version of minimalism to anyone else's.

If you have lessened down to what you feel is enough for you and your family members, then that's your type of minimalism. Your version of minimalism can change over time.

Comparing your type of minimalism to somebody else's version is like comparing apples to oranges. You're unique from every perspective. So there is little chance that your version of minimalism matches with other ones.

If somebody else decides how many books you should have, there is no minimalist authority or honor to offer you a ticket. It's merely a matter of finding out what your version of minimalism looks like for you.

Your goal of seeking minimalism is to give you space, flexibility, and time to enjoy your life and the people and things you value the most. However, you get to that point is what your type of minimalism looks like.

Learn from various other minimalists, after which you develop your own type of minimalism.

It can be useful to check out or see other individuals' versions of minimalism to influence and motivate your journey towards minimalism. It's great to learn what is helping them and what stumbling blocks they came across along the way. Also, listen to any type of minimalist living suggestions they have to share.

I think, seeing only how various other individuals "do things", minimalism is one of the best ways to find out more. It's a great way to challenge yourself to step out of your comfort zone and encourage yourself to the experiment of living with less.

You have to create your own version of minimalism. One that works for your family, your way of life, and your priorities. Rather than simply attempting to copy another person's type of minimalism. Find your own version of minimalism.

However, what if you are simply starting out on your minimalism journey and feeling overwhelmed without a set of policies or guidelines to comply with? Or suppose you've been reducing and decluttering for a certain time, but aren't sure about getting to a point of enough in your kind of minimalism?

With a little consideration and thought, you can easily figure out how you want your kind of minimalism to look like. Asking yourself some important questions will certainly help you get clarity regarding this fact, as well as what you'll need to do to get there.

Here are three questions to help you find your type of minimalism:

1. Why are you choosing minimalism?

First, consider what led you to minimalism and decluttering. What is motivating you to welcome minimalism?

Are you tired of investing the majority of your time dealing with "stuff" and want even more time and energy for your family members, hobbies, or pals? Or are you really feeling bogged down by your life and stuff, and looking for a way to free yourself?

There are many reasons that can lead you to minimalism. The initial step to figuring out only how you desire your type of minimalism to look is to be clear about what you desire to accomplish. Be clear about your objectives.

For me, I was so fed up with running after my kid when she was always entering every shelf, storage room, and cupboard she could reach. One day I realized I was investing so much time getting, doing away with, and organizing things I really did not enjoy or use. What was the point?! I wanted to invest less time managing stuff and more time appreciating my life and my household.

Give yourself the reasons that you are actually minimizing. Advising yourself can help you make tough decluttering decisions. Also, if you're decluttering and are feeling overwhelmed or tired, remembering why you're working so hard to accept minimalism can help you get inspired and on track.

2. What is very important to you?

Minimalism is the intentional promo?? Of the

important things we value most and the removal of anything that sidetracks us from it". Focus on this, before you can accept minimalism. First, you need to get clarified about what you, in fact, value most!

Possibly it's your family and being able to invest top quality time with them. It could be a hobby you like that you desire even more time for.

For me, being able to have more composure, energy, and time to provide for my family members is crucial. In order to do this, I need to have a house that is easy to keep. Then, I can conveniently remain on top of work and family chores to be able to invest top quality time enjoying my family members without really feeling stressed or overwhelmed with the mess in my house.

I want to offer my family the most effective version of myself, in terms of my time, energy, presence, attention, and composure; not what's leftover after I have actually spent most of my time handling stuff in our lives.

Again, this is something only you can choose and it will be different for each of us. You need to make sure for yourself what is important to you, and what you value most.

What is it you're attempting to make more time and room for in your life by embracing minimalism? Write it down to think on your own and help you stay determined and motivated on your journey.

3. What does the term "sufficient" look like for you?

This is something you need to figure out as you go through the procedure of decluttering your house. Start questioning what enough looks like for you, so you can let go of every little thing beyond what is enough.

Once again, only you will understand what works for you. Some individuals determine enough is possessing less than 100 ownerships. Others choose their place of sufficient is a lot more than that.

There's no right or wrong solution to what 'enough' appears like for you. It's merely finding out what is right for you. 'Enough' will mean only keeping things that add value to your life because you use them on a regular basis, or they make you happy. But once again, what suffices will be individual and unique to everyone.

After you have actually decided what enough looks like for you, it's also an excellent idea to question and test your suggestion of 'enough'.

For instance, sometimes we keep things since we have always had them and are simply used to them being there. Or perhaps something came as a set, so we think we need to keep the whole set.

An example of figuring out what is enough

Dishes are a wonderful example of this. When we got married, we had a set of recipes with 12 place setups. They all suit the cupboard easily and were a set, so I didn't consider decluttering them at first. Since we had a cupboard full of clean dishes, it was easy to use a brand- new plate or bowl any time we wanted to. This left us with plenty of filthy dishes every day.

I put half the place settings away only to try living with less. We have fewer filthy dishes each day simply due to the fact that there are fewer dishes, so we are a lot more cautious about how we use the dishes.

Obstacle and inquiry what is enough??

Often, we need to ask ourselves and even challenge ourselves to see if our place of enough is actually sufficient, or if we can do with less. Asking and questioning exactly how much you have and why you have it.

Be adaptable with your type of a basic minimal way of life

Addressing these three questions can help you find out how you desire your type of minimalism to look like. It is necessary to bear in mind that minimalism isn't something you obtain, and then you're done. It's a way of life you embrace and requires your ongoing focus, maintenance, and intent to sustain it. But answering these questions will help you remain concentrated and inspired to continue living and finding your own type of minimalism.

Your version of minimalism will change as your

life changes, and it is important to remember that Minimalism isn't static or unvarying. It moves and develops as your life changes and. Your response to these three questions will also change with time. Revisit these questions periodically to make sure your answers still relate to your life.

Addressing these questions is a great means to comprehend, clarify, and remind yourself what your type of minimalism looks like. Use these answers to resolve the difficult moments and celebrate the victories of living a life with less.

5
WHAT IS SIMPLE LIVING?

As my passion for simplifying our life expanded, I reviewed numerous blogs about basic living. Something that stood out to me is that there is no single interpretation of what simple living means. It means different things to different people — each person specifying it in a different way based upon their values and purposes.

None of these interpretations are incorrect or appropriate; any of those terms can mean many things to different individuals.

As I became a lot more serious about simplifying our house and lives, I needed to specify what 'simple living' means to me so that I could be clear about what type of life I am striving for.

I could not strive for somebody else's version of easy living. I needed to make a clear vision of what I wanted for our house, our family members, and our lives. Also, I needed to be clear about what practices to establish to live more securely.

To me, so much of easy living rests on less- both owning less and doing less, intentionally choosing to live a clean, minimalist, and slower life. I intend to make time and room for people and experiences that are most important for our family.

My type of simple living is composed of two broad ideas:

1. Possessing les
2. Doing less

To clarify, this is my vision for what a less complex life will appear like for our family members:

1. Organize Your Life by Possessing less Declutter and Accepting a Minimalist Lifestyle

Organizing life requires removing the excess so

that only the things we really like or need remain in our houses. It means viewing your home with an important eye to choose what does or does not add value to your life.

Keeping the things that add value. Just the important things you make use of and like.

You don't have to live without things that you love or so little that it makes life hard. The opposite is true; you live without all the excess and extra things that make life tougher.

"Enough" is when the things you have are what you make use of and love, nothing more. "Enough" is when you intentionally get rid of anything that isn't adding value to your life.

"Have absolutely nothing in your home that you do not know to be valuable or believe to be beautiful."

-- William Morris

Less Consumerism

You really feel the need to acquire less when you

choose to have less. You know that what you currently have is enough. You are able to move far from using shopping as a pastime or as an emotional Band-Aid.

Embracing basic living means deciding to quit meaningless intake that only winds up in the waste or contribute heap later. Shopping becomes a lot more intentional as our values shift to quality over quantity. You shop for only things you actually need and will certainly add value to your life, without the thrill of only buying something new.

Making this shift is when you've started decluttering and living a minimalist life. A large focus of basic living for me is to make sure I get rid of the excess and after that quit buying more!

Using what I already have

Again, by choosing to have less and buy less, you choose to find ways to recycle or re-purpose things you currently own.

It might take some creativity to find means to re-purpose what I currently have to solve the issue I'm dealing with. I want to change my mindset to think of new ways I can use what I already have and get something brand-new if I can't discover anything that works.

Being material with what we already have.

Eventually, the decision to have less comes down to being material and grateful for what we already have. We not only have enough, but we also have a lot more than enough.

Part of my journey to simple living is to move my point of view towards contentment and thankfulness. It's so easy to get caught up in the suggestion of having all the latest and best of everything. It's easy to believe that if you simply had the most recent whatever (device, garments, devices, etc.), after that, you would be happy.

Simple living changes our emphasis away from wanting a lot more, and brings it back to thankfulness, seeing that what we have is already enough.

2. Organize Your Life by Slowing Down and Doing Less Slowing down and doing less

A big part of living a less complex life to me

means slowing down and deliberately deciding exactly how we will certainly dedicate our time. It appears as though life is so stressful today.

As part of our journey to a simpler life, we want to reduce our workload and do less. We make it a point to enroll in fewer scheduled activities, and are discerning regarding the ones we do enroll in.

We want to make time and room for plenty of breaks and playtime for the kids. That's when the magic of childhood years occurs!

I do not wish to hurry with that or take that away from my children. It helps them to find ways to amuse themselves. I want them to discover the world and see what they uncover.

I want them to play and use their imaginations. That time is so priceless for children, and frequently it's infringed upon by way too many set-ups, structured activities.

Doing less reflects on our entire household. We wish to put in a great deal of time in our home together for everyone. Both my husband and I restrict the commitments we take on to give us a lot of time together as a family.

Another way we try to slow down is by focusing on cooking dishes and eating them together as family members, particularly supper. We aim for easy, well-balanced, and healthy dishes.

I am not an extremely adventurous cook, and my family isn't especially adventurous eaters. It works well to make our dishes made with simple ingredients. This way I prevent littering my kitchen with fancy & seldom used main ingredients.

Create your Vision of Simple Living

This is exactly how I define basic living and that's what I'm aiming to accomplish. For me, all it boils down to purposefully choosing to do and own less in order to create a simpler, extra-willful life.

If you are considering producing a less complex, extra-intentional life, I seriously suggest the very first step be defining what a deliberate or basic life means to you. Be clear about what you want simple living to look like in your life. Share your vision with your family and get their input. With a shared, clear vision, you are far more likely to reach your goals.

THINGS YOU GAIN WHEN YOU DEAL WITH LESS

It's not about what you're getting rid of when you are simplifying and choosing to live with less. The best part about organizing your life is what you get by releasing and choosing to deal with less. When you agree to let the clutter go, the distractions, the excess, and the busyness, you stand to acquire a lot more: even more time, more space, more flexibility, and eventually more peace.

Change your emphasis to what you'll gain, not what you're removing.

While you're in the procedure of decluttering and simplifying, a lot of the focus is on what you're getting rid of. There are other things; too much clutter, several commitments, also lots of distractions.

You begin getting rid of the mess, the excess, and the interruptions. It's very easy to forget that the entire point of deciding to live with less is about what you're making space for.

What you gain when you live with less is a lot more important than what you're letting go of. It's about choosing to have fewer things, so you can have even more life.

Things You Gain When You Cope With Less

Today I wish to share 4 things you can gain when you choose to simplify and live with less. These 4 things are what make the organizing journey worth it. They are what make it worth the time and initiative to remove the clutter and the distractions.

While you're simplifying and decluttering, rather than focusing on what you're getting rid of, releasing, or giving up, keeps your focus on what you're getting. When you have a focus on what you'll gain by letting go, it ends up being so much easier to let go of the clutter and interruptions.

Below are 4 amazing things you'll gain when you cope with less:

1. Time

Some take more time than others, but everything in your house calls for some of your time and energy. The fewer things you possess, the lesser of your time and energy are taken up handling your stuff. When things add value to your life, since you use them regularly or love them, it's okay when they take up some of your time and energy.

When you let go of things that do not add value to your life, you gain more energy and time to focus on what is crucial to you and what you value.

2. Room

As you remove the clutter and the excess from your home, you'll create space in your house. Rooms will be less crowded and cluttered. Closets and cupboards will have space. You'll add space to take a breath to your home.

Where there was once a mess, you'll get space. The room you can make use of for living and enjoying what you value most, as opposed to storing mess.

Beyond developing physical space for your house, you'll additionally add space to various other areas of your life.

Room in your timetable

You'll also give on your own the possibility to develop space in your timetable. Simplifying help, you identify what dedications, tasks, and responsibilities add value to your life, and which only add mess, interruption, and distraction.

As you begin to say "no" to the things in your routine that aren't adding value, you make room in your routine —giving you more chances to say yes to the tasks and dedications you love and add value to your life.

"Learn to say 'no' to the excellent so you can say 'yes' to the best."

~ John C Maxwell Space in your mind

A chaotic space leads to a messy mind. Mess, disturbances, and wastage of time mean that your mind can't rest. Rather, your mind is being drawn in several instructions, sidetracked, and simply trying to keep up.

Organizing your home and your routine enables you to get rid of the psychological clutter and gain clarity. It also reduces your stress levels and offers your body and mind space to remainder and recharge, without being disturbed by mess and disturbances.

. . .

3. Freedom

Choosing to live with fewer belongings allows you to take control of what fills your time and space. Instead of allowing excess, mess, and distractions to take up your time and space, you make intentional choices about what occupies your time and place. You also get the freedom to invest your time and energy in what is most important to you.

Simply, it could mean having even more time and energy for the tasks and individuals you enjoy. Because you tend to spend less time and energy handling the things you possess.

4. Tranquility

Ultimately, deciding to cope with less gives you the possibility to build an extra peaceful life. You're no longer desperately attempting to stay up to date with life and handling all your things and commitments. Rather, you can intentionally focus on what is crucial to you due to the fact that you have the time, space, and liberty to do which is why simplifying, decluttering, and minimalism are so fantastic. You can release a chaotic, stressful, excessively hectic, and frantic life, and instead create a calmer, extra deliberate, a lot more tranquil life.

Decluttering, simplifying, and choosing to deal with less has to do with so much more than having a clean home. That's a remarkable benefit! Choosing to cope with less has to do with making room for what you'll gain when you get rid of the clutter and distractions and that's what it's all about, choosing fewer things so you can have even more life!

6
MINDFULNESS

Practicing mindfulness is one of the ways I'm creating my vision for a simpler life. I am sharing these three means I'm creating time and space in our house and our lives to live more simply and mindfully.

What is Mindfulness?

Mindfulness is a term that is commonly used; however, can hold different meanings. I'm making use of the list below of definitions of mindfulness:

"Mindfulness is a state of active, open attention on the here and now. When you're conscious, you observe your ideas and feelings from a distance, without evaluating them as great or bad.

"Mindfulness is the standard human capacity to be totally alive, familiar with where we are and what we're doing, and not overly responsive or overwhelmed by what's going on around us."

Based on these definitions, there are 2 main things regarding mindfulness I will focus on:

1. Living in the moment
2. Preventing attachments to or reacting without intention to ideas and feelings

Staying Present

Practicing mindfulness looks like a simple suggestion, however that doesn't indicate it's simple! Focusing on and remaining in the here and now minute is really hard to practice consistently. It is easy to zone out or go through your everyday jobs on auto-pilot.

Mindfulness is everything about being willful with precisely how you invest your time and being an energetic participant in your life. Living in the moment and proactively paying attention to what is going on around you, requires you to re-train the way you act and think every day.

Living mindfully takes technique and purpose to cultivate. The great news is, the more you exercise mindfulness, the easier and even more natural it will certainly end up being.

Locating a Time Out to Act and React Purposefully

Another component of mindfulness is observing your feelings and thoughts, without judgment, and then letting those thoughts and feelings ended up being connected to them.

Living enough to know what you are thinking or really feeling can be difficult. It is tougher to recognize your feelings and thoughts and give yourself a minute to observe and reflect on them before reacting. Rather, making a mindful choice about how you will certainly react with an objective.

I find this particularly challenging while going to a house with toddlers. Parenting regularly tests my capacity to be alive enough to observe the method I'm really feeling and observing my initial reactions to scenarios before having that response. I usually feel tired, excessively needed, fagged out, and active; and it is a genuine challenge for me to observe my feelings before they appear as unfavorable responses.

My Mindfulness Method

Part of my goal in creating an easier life is to live even more intentionally. I want to organize our lives so there are fewer distractions to keep me from living in the moment. I don't want to allow life to pass me by while I'm busy cleaning up or hurrying from one task to the next. Rather, I want to live my life and live with my family.

Furthermore, I intend to produce space between my ideas, feelings, and reactions to the scenarios. I wish to be able to offer myself the space to pause and to react with purpose rather than out of habit.

Minimalism

Developing time and space to live mindfully is only one of the reasons I am focusing on organizing and minimalism, to begin with. Below are three key means I'm working to add both time and room to add mindfulness in my life.

Three Ways I'm Making Room for Mindfulness in My Life:

1. Clearing up my physical space

Clutter and much stuff, generally make me feel overloaded and anxious. When I feel overloaded with our space, it's extremely challenging to keep my focus on the present minute.

In addition, when I really feel bewildered by those excess "things" in our home, I find it a lot tougher to find that space in between my thoughts or feelings and my reactions. More frequently than not, my responses when I feel overwhelmed by mess and clutter are less than beneficial.

Choosing Fewer Things to Find More Peace

I have actually been making a conscious effort to get rid of the excess things in our house, maintaining only what we like and make use of. The stuff we bring into our houses occupies our time, especially when we do not understand it. We clean it, arrange it, store it, find it, and so on.

The fewer things I have in my house, the less time I have to spend dealing with them, and the more time I have to be present. The less time I invest tidying up the usual messes, the more time I have to be alive. It allows me to take a seat and play with my children without stressing over all the work that's not getting done.

The more, I do away with it, the extra calm and minimalist our environment is. In turn, the less worried and overloaded I feel. When I feel calmer, I am far better able to remain focused on the here and now minute. When I can be alive, I find it simpler to give myself a minute of time out between observing my ideas or feelings and responding.

This moment of time-out gives me the opportunity to respond in such a way that can have a favorable effect on my family members, instead of negatively reacting out of aggravation, stress to be minimal officially or bewilder.

fewer things = less stress and anxiety = a lot more presence = more tranquil = extra willful responses

1. A consistent and individual yoga and reflection method

I have actually practiced yoga for many years, yet the last number of years I expanded a consistent, day-to-day technique. And what a difference it's made! The physical method of yoga provides me the possibility to tune into my body and mind, observe only how I'm feeling and exactly how those feelings are manifested in my body and life. Practicing yoga exercise regularly is instructing me to be more in touch with and aware of my feelings and ideas, both on and off the floor covering.

Mindfulness in Yoga

Yoga exercise calls for mindfulness. As you move via the ??, you focus on the circulation of your breath. and connect your movements with your breath. Yoga exercise calls for emphasis, flexibility, and strength. When you are concentrated on matching your activities with your breath or remaining balance in a tough posture, mindfulness is vital. Without focusing on the here and now moment, you will most likely wind up dropping on your face!

You train both your body and mind to return to the present moment by concentrating on your breath. And yoga trains you to direct your focus to your breath to remain mindful and present.

Self-Care for Mindfulness

My yoga practice has taught me a lot about how to live more mindfully. Not only that, but an everyday yoga exercise practice has actually made me feel great. It helps to feel me stronger, and a lot more in shape than I have actually ever before felt before.

It's been such fantastic self-care, something I'm doing only for me that makes me feel excellent. The better I feel, the simpler it seems to remain alive.

Feeling much better also helps give me that moment of pause between seeing my feelings and responding. Then I can pick a more willful reaction.

Meditation for Mindfulness

I am currently dealing with setting a more constant meditation technique. I find it actually challenging to practice meditation daily. Know it is so vital to really feel a lot more calm, based, and mindful throughout the day.

Like yoga exercise, meditation teaches you to return your emphasis to your breath to remain present and release any diversions that show up. Beyond that, it's been proven that a regular reflection technique can make you a lot more conscious and happier generally.

I have actually been working hard to create an extra regular, everyday meditation practice. Not only is it tough to find time to rest by myself with two tiny kids around me, resting silently, staying present, and not being connected to ideas or concepts that come up is not something that really feels natural to me.

Keeping our timetable tranquil

As a family of introverts, most of us call for a great deal of silent, breaks to reenergize. Recognizing this about ourselves, we have actually made cautious options about how we dedicate our time and fill our routine. Having way too many commitments stresses me out and makes me really feel tired out and drained. When they are too constant or rushed, it also appears to confuse my children and takes the fun out of activities.

Getting to arrange plenty of breaks offers us the opportunity to notice what we are really feeling in the moment and only as necessary. With fewer commitments and tasks, I can adjust our days to match our needs and moods. Leaving unfilled time in our timetable is vital to be able to do this. When I see we need a silent day to recharge, it's easy to do since we have space in our days and routine.

It's difficult to remain in the alive moment when you really feel rushed and frazzled, constantly preparing and planning for the next activity. Fewer tasks and even more breaks allow us all to be a lot more present in the minute and conscious of our activities, feelings, and ideas.

Utilizing Mindfulness to Produce Better Days

These are three key methods I am creating both time and space to live more mindfully. I find the days where I have the ability to feel more alive in the tasks we are doing and find that quick moment of pause between noticing my thoughts or emotions and responding to them, to be better days. Days where I go to bed feeling material and relaxed. Knowing I used my time intentionally and fostered a strong connection between our families, they are the sort of days I desire even more. The activities over are only how I wish to continue living more mindfully and be productive even more of those days.

Minimalism and Mindfulness

I shared ways I'm making time and room in my life to practice mindfulness. This made me thinking about the connection between minimalism and mindfulness.

I realized minimalism is not only a means to produce time and room for mindfulness. Minimalism is actually a mindfulness technique in itself, and in fact, mindfulness sustains and encourages it in return. Minimalism and mindfulness make an excellent set! I've assembled a list of four means minimalism and mindfulness motivate and support each other.

What is Mindfulness?

Below is a quick description of what mindfulness suggests in this chapter.

As I mentioned in my previous chapter, mindfulness is a method that includes:

1. concentrating on staying alive in the moment, and in turn,

2. creating space, or a moment of pause, in between your ideas or feelings and your responses to them

Mindfulness is about remaining focused and

present within yourself, to bring more calm, existence, and objectivity into your life.

Minimalism and Mindfulness

To me, minimalism and mindfulness have a circular relationship. Each creating problems to help in the various others.

By focusing on being alive and mindful, we end up being a lot more willful about what uses up our time and space. To be able to stay present in the minute through mindfulness, we intend to eliminate any type of things or dedications that distract us or hinder our capacity to remain alive. This consequently encourages us to let go of more, and accept minimalism even more.

Both minimalism and mindfulness encourage, sustain, and inspire various ways to create and expand in our lives.

In a lot of methods, minimalism and mindfulness educate us on most of the same lessons. Below are four means of minimalism and mindfulness job in the direction of and with each various other. Demonstrating only how minimalism promotes more mindfulness in your life, and how mindfulness is an important component to accepting a minimalist frame of mind.

4 Ways Minimalism and Mindfulness Make a Superb Pair

1. Releasing add-ons

Minimalism entails decluttering our rooms and

choosing to keep only the things we use on a regular basis and/or love. Throughout this procedure, we discover to let go of our accessories to the things we possess. Recognizing the products we have are there to offer us or add value to our lives, and discovering to let go of anything that doesn't fit.

Minimalism requires us to evaluate knowingly what we have and why we have it. Minimalism shows us to become a lot more conscious and willful about what things we help in our homes.

By accepting minimalism, owning less, and simplifying, we produce time and space to come to be extra-mindful. Enabling us to be present at the moment.

Minimalism also reminds us that things we have are not what issue most in life. Releasing anything no longer, including value to our lives, adds more vital things like individuals we share our lives with and our experiences throughout our days.

Mindfulness in our heads. Minimalism in our houses.

Minimalism and mindfulness both promote the concept and instruct us of to devoid of attachments.

Mindfulness shows and urges us to remain present and to see our ideas and feelings. Rather, mindfulness educates us to discover ideas or feelings; after that, allow them to go in order to remain centered and calm.

Minimalism focuses on non-attachment in our

houses. With minimalism, you observe and pay close focus to the things in your environment.

2. Remaining in todays' moment

An important element of mindfulness is remaining alive, and focusing on living in the minute.

Minimalism urges us only to help things in the houses we currently use and/or like. Instead, maintaining only the things, we make use of and like in our lives right currently, in the alive moment.

Past and future clutter

Much of the clutter falls right into the past or future groups.

Past mess is items that we made use of to love, yet our interests or demands have changed now. We use or enjoy them no more, and even things that we never made use of or enjoyed. But we tend to shut out of responsibility, guilt, laziness, indecisiveness, or behavior.

Or perhaps we have strategies to make use of the item "someday." Future mess occurs when we encourage ourselves to help something since we see the possibility of only how we could use it.

Minimalism and Mindfulness: Focus on the present

Minimalism changes our focus to the alive minute. Instead, maintaining only what we will actually use and enjoy today.

In the same way, mindfulness focuses on

remaining present and living in the minute. By embracing minimalism, only having the things you enjoy and use in your present season of life in your home. It is less complicated to remain in the present scenario.

3. Having less allows you to be much more deliberate and alive with your time

Along with liberating your room by only possessing what you use and like in present, embracing minimalism likewise liberates your time and permits you to be extra alive in your lives and deliberate with exactly how you invest your time.

Rather than allowing our "things" to rule our lives and determine how we invest our time. After embracing minimalism, you no longer need to invest the majority of your time taking care of your belongings. Which after that produces time and space to be a lot more present in your life.

Applying minimalism and mindfulness to your time

Commonly simplifying and reducing your room inspires you to use minimalism in various other areas of your life. Likewise, by concentrating on simplifying your routine, you can get even more time and flexibility to live in the alive moment.

Minimalism motivates you to construct both time and space into your life, purposefully allowing you a lot more liberty and opportunities to be willful and remain alive in every means.

4. Focusing on the journey, not completion outcome

Minimalism is a lot more about the journey as you practice, explore, and implement it into your life. And it is less about the end outcome of having a clutter-free room.

There truly is no end goal or finish line of minimalism that you get to one day and is done. Rather, it's a way of living you select to exercise each day.

You select to live and be content with less due to the value of living with less development. So, you choose to only keep things in your home that add value to your life, and make the option to be deliberate, not only with your space, yet likewise with your time.

You make choices each day to exercise minimalism. Along the journey of those daily options is where you experience the advantages of minimalism.

Mindfulness is additionally about the journey, rather than an end goal or destination. Just like minimalism, you switch to practice mindfulness on a daily basis.

It suggests making an aware, day-to-day initiative to be more alive at the moment and showing on your own to discover yourself, space, and time awareness to see your thoughts and feelings.

Minimalism and mindfulness: altering and progressing journeys

Both minimalism and mindfulness are procedures and trips, always changing and evolving as your life adjustments and progresses. What your type of both minimalism and mindfulness appear like today might be different from how they looked last year or the upcoming years.

The essential to both is the everyday deliberate selections you make. These small, willful everyday selections, to live minimally and mindfully, after that amount to produce large changes in your life in time.

Minimalism and Mindfulness: an excellent set

Minimalism is an outstanding way to practice mindfulness and bring even more of it into our lives. It is a way to remove our time, space, and minds of unneeded clutter, which after that allows us to live even more mindfully every now and then, continue to be calm and centered and stay clear of reacting without idea or objective.

In turn, living mindfully offers itself to accepting a minimal state of mind. The more alive you are, the easier it is to identify what adds value and what doesn't.

Minimalism develops time and space for mindfulness. and afterward, mindfulness subsequently helps relocate us in the direction of a state of mind that accepts and urges minimalism.

7

THE MINIMALIST MINDSET SHIFT

Minimalism is greater than decluttering and organizing alone. Those are necessary components of the minimalist trip. Embracing minimalism includes moving the means that you believe to have a minimalist state of mind.

Minimalism has to do with deciding to possess less, rather than decluttering more frequently. It has to do with altering your view of what you have and why you own it. This minimal attitude shift occurs in a progressive and discrete way in small methods. Until eventually, you check out and realize your relationship with "stuff" has altered. You have a different point of view. Your journey towards minimalism has actually altered your way of thinking, in what I like to call the 'minimalist attitude shift'.

My Own Minimalist Way of Thinking Shift

My spouse was going to hockey with some good friends and I had a visit the following day. So we decided to make a mini-getaway out of it. We live in a tiny town with restricted purchasing alternatives. When we went to the city earlier, we generally had a lengthy purchasing list of things. We "needed" and invested the whole time running from shop to shop.

Activities as opposed to purchasing

This journey was different. While we did do a little buying, without even realizing or meaning it, experiences and activities together ended up being the emphasis of our weekend break.

We went to a big shopping mall that has a resort, theme park, and various other amusement options in addition to the shops. I had plenty of things I was preparing to purchase, a brand-new pair of shoes for me and some summer season garments for the kids. We were most likely to a couple of stores, but the kids promptly spotted the amusement park trips. We told them they can ride a few trips; however, we ended up spending the remainder of the mid-day there.

The children had a blast, and it was such a fun and spontaneous way to spend the mid-day. It was a wonderful change.

It's the little things

We did this primarily because we were worn out and really did not really feel like going out once more. The children assumed it was the largest reward ever before. It advised me easy things can be so much enjoyable for children.

After dinner, we went swimming in the hotel pool. It was such an enjoyable, straightforward day. Absolutely nothing fancy or elaborate. However, all of us had a good time with each other.

Our attitude had altered

En route to our house, my husband and I reviewed the reality that we invested during DOING things rather than BUYING things, and what a distinction is made. We both noticed only how much nicer this journey was and how much fun it was. As I thought of it, I recognized our attitude has changed and changed. We were now living with a minimalist state of mind.

Having less, Not Removing Extra

Changing your frame of mind can often be the greatest hurdle in the direction of minimalism for a lot of us. We declutter and remove our houses and are delighted to welcome a more minimalist way of living. Then a couple of months later on, we've obtained a bunch of brand-new things to take the location of the old. We declutter and purge, and the cycle continues. Without altering the means we think about "stuff". Yet, adopting a minimal attitude, it's difficult to make a big shift to minimalism.

Of course, individuals who completely embrace minimalism need to remove and declutter periodically. When you have embraced the concept of minimalism in a holistic way, the method you believe modifications.

Observing this modification to a minimal mindset we'd experienced throughout our weekend break getaway. It paved ways of thinking about the means minimalism changes the method you assume as you take on a minimal mindset.

The Minimalist Mindset Shift

Ways Minimalism Changes the Method You Assume.

Right here are minimal state of mind changes I've experienced since embracing life with less:

1. Value experiences over physical things

Once you have actually committed to dealing with less, you start seeking ways to spend your time, not simply what you can buy next. You would rather invest your time and money doing something to produce memories, not add clutter to your life. Experiences, journeys, and activities end up being more important than obtaining more things.

2. Stop purchasing things you do not need

As you embrace minimalism, you come to be more deliberate about what you bring into your space. You fell short of (or at least decrease, due to the fact that learning to embrace coping with less is a procedure and will not occur overnight) acquiring things just to please your need for something brand-new.

Instead, you only get things you have considered very carefully and made a decision that will add value to your life. You start purchasing less and being more deliberate about what you do buy.

Your investing habits generally change after the minimal way of thinking changes. You prioritize investing money on experiences and activities as opposed to buying more "stuff."

You quit seeing shopping as a leisure activity and begin to seek new pastimes or hobbies that add value to your life, make you happy which aren't focused on consumerism or obtaining a lot more.

3. Become a tough and willful gatekeeper concerning what you enable into your house and your life.

In your difficult job of decluttering, removing, and lessening your house, the last thing you want to do is load it right back up with things. Understanding how much work is required to drop your excess stuff is an excellent inspiration to stop unnecessary products from entering your house once again, to begin with.

Quitting unneeded or undesirable things from coming right into your home in the very first location. Your concentration shifts so that you are able to be much more willful and careful regarding what you allow in your room in the initial location.

4. Concentrate on having less instead of decluttering more frequently

After the minimalist state of mind changes, you stop the cycle of decluttering, then purchasing even more, then decluttering again. Nevertheless, the moment and effort you put into decluttering your house, you do not wish to wind up right back where you began.

After the minimal attitude shift, you understand that owning less is a lot easier and much more beneficial than decluttering more. Your emphasis modifications and you actually WANT to have less due to the value it brings to your life.

5. Become a lot more deliberate with your time

Minimalism is not only about your "things." It surpasses physical things and changes the means you invest your time.

You start saying no to commitments that don't align with what you value, and stating no to commitments that take too much time far from what you DO value. You identify that your time is your most valuable resource and become more intentional with exactly how you spend it.

The minimalist frame of mind change alters what you enable to occupy both your room and your time. You become extra willful with both your time and space.

6. Realize happiness does not come from "things."

After you accept the minimalist attitude, you no more seem like you constantly need more. You no more tie your happiness to what you possess, assuming if once you get the latest and biggest "thing" you'll rejoice. You stop believing you'll enjoy it as soon as you make your next purchase.

Your joy and self-respect are no longer dependent on what you own. You recognize the things you own are here to offer you, either by working or bringing you joy. What you have does not specify you as an individual or identify your happiness.

7. Stop comparing yourself to others based on what you own.

As you accept the minimalist frame of mind, you let go of the idea of "keeping up with the Joneses." You also make the intentional choice only to help what you like and use.

You feel content with your valuables, understanding they bring value to your life rather than burdening you. Keeping that, you no more compare what you own to what other people possess due to the fact that it matters not. Your belongings do not specify your life or your social values. Due to the fact that possessing less makes your life better, you are material with less. Contrast based upon what individuals very own becomes meaningless.

8. Stop letting anxiety or a shortage frame of mind guideline what stays in your home.

You stop maintaining things "just in case" or since you could need it at some point. You realize only how rarely those "simply in situation" times actually take place. On the odd occasions, you discover yourself without something you might make use of; you realize there are several prospective solutions.

Rather than holding on to a whole lot of stuff only in case, you look for choices for things you need. Perhaps you have one more item you can use in its location. Or probably you can get the thing from a friend. Sometimes you can, in fact, do without the thing entirely and recognize you didn't need it nevertheless, and often, if you can discover no other alternative, you might need to get something you formerly did away with.

Yet those times really are uncommon. and if you ask me, the room and freedom you get from getting rid of a lot of unneeded mess are definitely valued at the rate of having to potentially re-buy the weird thing if you ever need it.

9. Realize arranging is not the answer.

I believe Many of us are guilty of assuming we need to arrange when actually we only have too much stuff to start with!

The things are all still there and will ultimately make their means out of your arranged system and create the exact same anxiety in your life. only after that will you free up both time and room in your house and your life.

Steady Shift.

Bear in mind that welcoming minimalism is just a process; these changes to a minimalist state of mind don't take place overnight. The majority of us have actually spent a lot of our lives being told more is much better and being pestered with consumerism. It takes time and initiative to change the method we assume. And a few of these changes will certainly come extra for you, unlike others. Over time, a lot more you embrace minimalism as a lifestyle, the extra your state of mind shifts to accept a minimalist state of mind.

8
WHY HIGHLY SENSITIVE PEOPLE NEED MINIMALISM

People who are highly sensitive feel the results of chaos and clutter particularly. Too many sensory details, including visual mess, can make delicate individuals feel overwhelmed and stressed out.

I already knew clutter makes me feel uncertain and worried. But after realizing that I am an extremely delicate person, it came to be a lot more crucial to strive for a basic, and minimalist life. Actually, highly delicate people NEED minimalism in every sphere of their lives.

What is an Extremely Sensitive Person?

Highly Sensitive People is a relatively brand-new space of research, with Dr. Elaine Aron pioneering it in the 1990s. Dr. Aron estimates Highly Sensitive People make up around 15-- 20% of the populace.

Until a few years earlier, I didn't also understand what a Highly Delicate Person was. One day I review an article regarding it and it was as if I was reading about myself! I recognized many things which I assumed to affect my very own little affectations. Things other people experienced, and even better; there was even a name for it! It was an alleviation to learn that individuals experienced these same things.

After understanding being a Highly Sensitive Person is a "point," it became easier to recognize and accept these aspects of myself and make changes in my life where feasible. I perceived that, by accepting them as part of who I am with them, rather than versus them; I might live a better, calmer life.

Characteristics of Very Sensitive Individuals

These are some common features of Very Delicate Individuals. The more of these things you associate with, the higher the possibility that you are an Extremely Sensitive Individual.

1. Sensory details easily overwhelms you

Things like loud audios, bright lights, solid scents, or uncomfortable textile structures can confuse and agitate a Highly Sensitive Person. Busy atmospheres or big groups have the very same effect.

2. Multi-tasking stress and anxieties you out

Extremely Delicate Individuals feel stressed out, overloaded, and nervous if they have a whole lot to do in a brief quantity of time. Having excessive to do, being overly active, or hurrying leaves an extremely delicate person sensation worn down and overwhelmed.

3. Physical violence in films, TV programs, or media deeply disturbs you

Seeing violence in TV shows, movies or news stories deeply distress and interrupts Highly Delicate Individuals. It's tough for them to get the image or concept of it out of their minds. They can feel unsettled about it for weeks afterward too.

4. You need silent time alone after a busy day

After a frustrating or active day, Highly Sensitive Individuals find themselves desperate for some silent time. Very Delicate People need time and space to shut the world out and recharge.

5. You thoroughly prepare your days to stay clear of overwhelming circumstances

Extremely Sensitive Individuals work hard to plan and schedule their days to stay clear of situations that overwhelm or upset them. They make certain to offer themselves enough time to complete tasks. and avoid needing to do greater than one task at the same time or in a short amount of time whenever possible.

6. You are particularly sensitive to the impacts of high levels of caffeine or appetite

Highly Delicate Individuals often tend to feel the effects of high levels of caffeine, feeling skittish or unsteady after consuming it. Their bodies additionally often tend to be sensitive to cravings. When they come starving, it significantly influences their mood and capacity to focus or complete tasks.

7. You have an intricate internal dialogue and creative imagination

Very Sensitive Individuals commonly find themselves getting lost in their thoughts and have a complex and deep inner life.

Very Delicate People tend to replay and assess discussions and experiences in their minds. They usually look at all the various feasible outcomes that could have occurred in their mind. Very Sensitive Individuals are commonly told they fret way too much, or over-think things.

The other side of this is they likewise tend to be imaginative. They have deep creative imaginations and invest a lot of time thinking about creative and new suggestions.

8. People frequently define you as overly delicate or shy

Highly Delicate Individuals are still not well recognized and are typically mislabeled. They are usually told they are being delicate or extremely psychological. Or perhaps that they need to condition or get thicker skin. They are also mislabeled as timid at times since they need to hang around alone and stay clear of some over-stimulating situations.

9. You tend to discover details in your setting others miss

Highly Delicate People tend to be extremely

watchful of their surroundings, discovering details others may miss out on.

10. You easily notice emotions of the others

Extremely Sensitive People tend to pick up on the state of mind and feelings of individuals around them. They might also handle the emotions of people around them at times. This is one-factor busy settings, and social situations can be tiring for Extremely Delicate Individuals.

11. Change is specifically challenging and distressing for you

Most Highly Sensitive Individuals have an everyday regimen they comply with feeling grounded and stay clear of feeling overwhelmed. When they experience modification, favorable, and even exciting changes, they commonly feel uncertain and overwhelmed by the change. Highly Delicate People also usually call for longer to adjust to changes in their lives than other people.

Searching For Ways to Deal as a Very Delicate Person

Various things can overwhelm a Highly Sensitive Individual. The crucial to flourishing as a Highly Sensitive Person is locating healthy and balanced ways to handle things that overwhelm you, and job to restrict or regulate your exposure to things that make you bewildered.

There are some frustrating aspects and scenarios an Extremely Delicate Person has no control over.

There are some things we can control. Among the most important things, we can control are our house and the space inside it.

A place to wait and recharge. This works not only for Highly Delicate Individuals but also for any person.

Why Extremely Sensitive People Need Minimalism?

Minimalism and decluttering are so crucial for Highly Delicate People. Clutter in our houses adds in the outside stimulation that makes us feel overwhelmed and stressed out. A chaotic space full of too much stuff can make anyone feel unsettled. Especially a Highly Sensitive Individual

Clutter and well many other things add to the sensory info overload that can be overwhelming for a Very Sensitive Person. Mess makes it challenging for Extremely Delicate Individuals to unwind or rest elsewhere. Because they are bombarded with also much sensory information.

Currently think of an area with very little clutter, clear surface areas, and space to breathe. A space like this produces feelings of leisure, visibility, and calm. Having a clutter-free space with clear surfaces gives a location for your eyes and mind to remainder.

A tranquil and clean atmosphere helps to help our minds tranquil and minimalist. This is particularly true for Highly Sensitive People. Minimalism permits Extremely Sensitive People to develop the atmosphere they need to relax, kick back and charge. Particularly after dealing with the world and all its sensory overload throughout the day.

I'm an Extremely Delicate Individual ... and that's ALRIGHT!

In some cases, being a Very Sensitive Person can turn to appear like an adverse point. When we are told we are also sensitive, over-think things, or need to toughen up, it suggests being an Extremely Sensitive Person is a poor thing. Like it's a character problem we need to fix or get rid of to be a much more successful individual.

After learning even more about Highly Sensitive Individuals, I currently understand it is simply the method we are. It's neither negative nor good; it's simply that we are. There are advantages and drawbacks to being an Extremely Delicate Individual. Equally, as there are to almost any personality type. The key is finding means to improve the advantages and support yourself through the disadvantages.

As an example, Extremely Sensitive Individuals tend to be creative, empathetic, caring, and understanding. these are some aspects to celebrate indeed. On the other hand, Highly Delicate People can feel tired out and overwhelmed conveniently, deal with modification, and may come to be "angry." These are elements of being an Extremely Delicate Individual that can have adverse impacts on your life. However, you can handle them by recognizing, embracing, and accounting for these parts of your personality.

The more I find out to accept these inherent characteristics and not fight against being an Extremely Delicate Person. A much easier and extra tranquil life has to take place.

Minimalism is among the Trick Ways I Manage Being an Extremely Delicate Individual.

Several things can overwhelm a Highly Delicate Individual. The crucial to growing as a Highly Delicate Person is locating healthy methods to manage things that overwhelm you, and job to restrict or control your exposure to things that make you overwhelmed.

There are some overwhelming aspects and circumstances an Extremely Delicate Person has no control over. There are some things we can regulate. One of the most important things we can manage is our house and the space inside it.

We have the option to build a house that can be our resort intentionally. This uses not only for Highly Sensitive Individuals but for any individual.

Why Very Sensitive People Required Minimalism

Minimalism and decluttering are so important for Extremely Sensitive People. Clutter in our houses includes the external stimulus that makes us feel overloaded and worried. A messy room loaded with excessive stuff can make anybody feel unsettled. Clutter and way too many things contribute to the sensory info overload that can be overwhelming for a Very Delicate Individual. A cluttered environment provides our eyes and our minds fewer possibilities to rest. There are merely a lot of things to look at and take in. Because they are pounded with many sensory details, mess makes it hard for Extremely Delicate Individuals to relax or loosen up.

Now imagine an environment with really little mess, clear surfaces, and space to breathe. A space similar to this creates feelings of openness, calm, and leisure. Having a clutter-free space with clear surfaces offers a location for your eyes and mind to rest.

A tranquil and clean environment helps to maintain our minds tranquil and minimalist. This is particularly true for Extremely Sensitive People. Minimalism enables Very Delicate People to produce the atmosphere they need to relax, loosen up, and charge absolutely. Particularly after encountering the world and all its sensory overload throughout the day.

I'm a Highly Sensitive Individual ... and That's ALRIGHT!

Sometimes being a Very Delicate Person can be made to appear like an unfavorable point. When we are told we are delicate, over-think things, or need to condition, it suggests being a Very Sensitive Person is a negative point. Like it's a character defect, we should get rid of or deal with it to be an extra successful person.

After discovering even more about Very Delicate People, I now recognize it is only the method we are. There are benefits and disadvantages to being a Highly Delicate Individual.

Very Delicate People tend to be innovative, understanding, caring, and understanding. All of which are things to commemorate. On the other hand, Highly Delicate Individuals can feel tired out and overwhelmed within a while, fight with change, and easily become "angry." These are facets of being a Highly Delicate Person that can have negative effects on your life. You can manage them by comprehending, welcoming, and accounting for these parts of your character.

I learn to embrace these natural personality types and not battle against being a Highly Delicate Person; the less complicated and extra relaxed life has ended up being.

Minimalism is among the Key Ways I Cope with Being a Highly Sensitive Person.

Learning more about being an Extremely Sensitive Individual gave me more motivation to declutter, lessen, and simplify our lives.

I understand I need our house to be a calm and clutter-free environment for me to be able to remain peaceful amidst the more than stimulating turmoil and hours of the outside world and life with toddlers. Because I'm a Very Sensitive Person, simplifying our house and life has had a massive positive impact on me. This showed me that the course of simplifying and reducing was the ideal one for me to be on.

9

QUOTES TO MOTIVATE YOU TO DECLUTTER

Words are effective. They have the ability to motivate us, inspire us, and push us to do something about it. Check out these 25 straightforward quotes to motivate and encourage you on your journey if you're in the process of decluttering and organizing your house!

These easy quotes are the ones that have actually gotten hold of me and inspired me. Most notably, the quotes regarding organizing life that I return to time and time again to remind myself why organizing and choosing to live with fewer leads to a life of more of what matters most to me.

I have actually always loved accumulating quotes and words that influence me. By sharing many of the much-loved basic living quotes I have actually collected throughout the years. I wish they inspire and encourage you as you organize your life as long as they have for me!

Use them whenever you need to find inspiration and motivation in the direction of simplifying and decluttering your home and your life!

25 easy quotes to influence you to declutter & simplify your life!

1. "Have absolutely nothing in your house that you do not seem to be helpful or believe to be gorgeous."

~ William Morris.

This is one of my preferred straightforward living quotes. It solves to the heart of what should be allowed to remain in our houses. Advising us only to maintain what adds value to our lives.

2. "Love people, make use of things. The opposite never ever functions."

~ The Minimalists.

Yes to this! Simplifying and minimalism have to do with a lot greater than only doing away with "things." Minimalism has to do with getting clear on your priorities so you can make sure your energy, time, and space line up with those top priorities. It's about prioritizing individuals we like, not the right stuff we possess.

3. "My goal is no more to get more done, but rather to have less to do.".

~ Francine Jay, Miss Minimalist.

Such an effective suggestion on moving your expectations and top priorities. Instead of attempting to get even more done, objective to have less to do.

Think about only how much of your day you invest in managing the stuff you own. Working to generate income to get it, looking for it, organizing it, selecting it up, seeking it, repairing it, cleansing it, restructuring it, and so on

. Clear the clutter, the distractions, and the useless. Work on your own breathing space -- in your schedule, in your house, and in your days. Decluttering your house, your schedule, your commitments and your time isn't to make sure that you can get more done. It's to ensure that you have less to do, to begin with!

4. "The starting step in crafting the life you want is to eliminate everything you don't."

~ Joshua Becker.

Wise words to obey. Find out which issues are the most to you. After that, eliminate anything that does not straighten with what matters most to you, or even worse, sidetracks you from what matters most.

Uncertain of what matters most to you? Begin by removing the mess, the excess, and the interruptions from your house and life. Notice what's left. That's what is very important to you, what makes you happy, and what lights you up.

Do away with the clutter and give yourself freedom, space, and time to use and appreciate what is very important.

5. "The ability to organize ways to get rid of the

unneeded to make sure that the required might talk.".

~ Hans Hofmann.

Organizing can feel complex when you're in the trenches, choosing after the decision regarding what to keep and what to remove. It all boils down to this-- getting rid of the clutter and distractions from your life so you have the energy, time, and space to focus on what you value the most.

6. "The question of what you wish to own is really the concern of how you want to live your life."

~ Marie Kondo, The Life-altering Magic of Tidying Up.

What you choose to have doesn't only use up your space; it additionally uses up your time, and what takes up your time amounts to only how you live your life.

Do not assume what you're getting rid of when you're decluttering. Instead, think of what you're choosing to maintain and ask yourself if it will contribute to the life you wish to live.

7. "Your house is a living space, not a storage room."

~ Francine Jay, The Happiness of less

Such a fantastic suggestion that your house ought to be a location loaded with life, not a location loaded with "stuff." So commonly, we hold on to things we used to use or like, or things we hope to use someday, or perhaps only things we assumed we would certainly use or enjoy; yet, do not.

Clear the mess and produce a house loaded with less stuff, and more living!

8. "Clutter smothers. Simplicity breathes."

~ Terry Guillemets

Mess and too many things evaluate you down. Our pieces of stuff are not passive; it proactively extracts from us. Stuff takes our room, our time, our energy, our freedom, and our tranquility.

Cleaning the mess and the extra from your life adds some breathing space to your house and your life. Eliminate the stuff you do not make use of, need, or perhaps like, after that take a deep breath and delight in the room and breathing space you've developed!

9. "Minimalism isn't about removing things you like. It's about detaching the things that divert you from the things you enjoy."

~ Joshua Becker, The Minimalist house

Minimalism is not about restriction, deprivation, or doing away with things you love. Rather, it's about identifying what is very important to you. Then removing the distractions, the clutter, and the excess that keep you from concentrating your time, energy, and interest on the things you like.

Minimalism gives you the opportunity to delight in and value things you like a lot more!

10. "The secret of joy, you see, is not found in looking for a lot more, but in creating the capacity to delight in less."

~ Socrates

You'll constantly be going after the following reason if you spend your life going after extra. When you shift your emphasis to what you currently begin and have to see exactly how little you actually need to have a satisfied, and complete life. You can stop hanker after gaining much more. You can discover contentment and happiness in the little things!

11. "Minimalism is not about having less. It has to do with making room for even more of what matters."

Minimalism is not about having less for the sake of having less. Rather, it has to do with eliminating the unwanted, the mess, and the disturbances from your house and your life. So you have even more time, energy, and space now to focus on what issues are most to you.

Minimalism doesn't need to look at a certain means, comply with another person's policies, or satisfy someone else's criteria. Figure out what matters most to you. Create more time and space for those things in your life.

12. "The very best things in life aren't things."

This is one more wonderful suggestion and one of my much-loved basic living quotes. When it boils down to it, one of the most precious along with crucial, indicate us, typically aren't "things" whatsoever. Generally, it's the memories we have, the experiences we have, in fact, lived, and the people we enjoy that issue greater than anything.

13. "It is the terrific, basic things of life which are the genuine ones nevertheless."

~ Laura Ingalls Wilder

Life doesn't have to splurge to be terrific. Frequently, the straightforward minutes are the ones we remember and value a great deal of.

14. "Thanks, opens the volume of life. It changes what we have right into enough, and extra."

~ Tune Beattie

Organizing and minimalism are everything about finding your space "adequate." When you concentrate on gratitude and locating this location of enough is so much simpler.

Appreciating and noticing what currently loads your life makes it so less complicated to move your viewpoint from desiring much more, newer, much better, etc. to coming to be content with what you have.

Gratefulness helps you see the value of the things you have in your life so you can stop feeling the need to get even more and release what isn't adding value to your life.

15. "A house with less possessions is much more roomy, a lot more calming, and much more focused on the people that live inside it."

~ Joshua Becker

Organizing and decluttering ended up being a lot less complicated when you shift your emphasis from what you're doing away with, and rather, focus on what you are acquiring. Making the choice to own fewer "things" provides you the chance to enjoy even more life in your house!

16. "There are 2 ways to be rich: one is by acquiring much, and the other is by wanting little."

~ Jackie French Koller

We live in a consumer-driven society. Embracing

an easier life enables you to live an abundant life by being content with less.

17. "Edit your life often and ruthlessly. It's your masterpiece, after all."

~ Nathan W. Morris

You are in charge of what loads your space and occupies your time. Remove the mess, the excess, and the diversions to see to it your life is the life you want to be living.

18. "Fill your life with experiences, not things. Have stories to inform, not things to show."

Research has shown that spending your money and time on experiences as opposed to product ownerships brings much longer enduring happiness and contentment with your life.

Prioritizing experiences over properties develops enduring memories, constructs partnerships, and extra.

All without adding the stress of at some point ending up with a house full of "stuff" and mess.

19. "Exactly how we invest our days is, obviously, exactly how we spend our lives."

~ Annie Dillard

As soon as in a while or every so typically, our lives are not made up of the things we do. Rather, the amount of our lives originates from the routines and practices we duplicate every day, day in day out.

20. "Minimalism is the willful promo of things we most value and the removal of anything that distracts us from it."

~ Joshua Becker, Simplify

Be clear about what you value most. detach anything from your space, time, and life that doesn't line up with what you value a lot.

If your type of minimalism looks various from a person else's, do not worry. Most of us value different things, so minimalism can look various for all of us! Instead, use minimalism as a device to give you the liberty to focus on what is crucial to you.

21. "I do not say no because I am so busy. I say no because I do not want to be so busy."

~ Courtney Carver

'Saying no to some things' gives you the possibility to say 'yes' to the most vital things in your life. It gives you the opportunity to enjoy and value what is important to you extra since you aren't also hectic, also sidetracked, or merely also worn down to appreciate it.

Give yourself some break and breathing space in your days. Say no to some things to save your time and energy so you have the ability to say yes to things you like and value.

This is another one of my much-loved straightforward living quotes and something I advise myself usually so I can remember to save my "yeses" for things that matter a lot.

22. "Outer order contributes to internal calm."

~ Gretchen Rubin, Outer Order, Inner Calmness

For a lot of us, the atmosphere we are surrounded by can have a large effect on only how we really feel. A chaotic setting can make us feel stressed, unsettled, grouchy, and unproductive. An organized, clutter-free space can help us feel peaceful, grounded, kicked back, clear-headed, and better.

I understand this is certainly real for me! Only how around you?

23. "Clutter is not only stuff on your floor covering; it's anything that stands between you and the life you intend to be living."

~ Peter Walsh

Decluttering and organizing are about a lot more than making it easier to help your house clean and tidy. From your bank account to your state of mind and expectation on life, decluttering can influence your entire life.

If you are going to allow go of the mess, the excess, and the diversions in your life, there are numerous advantages awaiting you. Including the capability to produce the life you wish to be living!

24. "Having a simplified, minimalist house actually is a form of self-care."

~ Emma Scheib

Self-care doesn't always mean bubble bathrooms and face masks. Often self-care means doing tough things or things you do not actually wish to do yet know that they will enrich your life, happiness, health, and/or wellness. and often, self-care adds doing things you could not even think of as self-care initially-- like decluttering your house!

Decluttering and simplifying your house and your life can be a crucial form of self-care for many of us. It permits us to stay in a space that nurtures us and supplies a sanctuary to rest and kickback. As opposed to a messy, unpleasant house that contributes to our anxiety and gives us an order of business that feels never-ending.

Decluttering doesn't solve all of life's troubles. It definitely gets rid of a large source of stress in our lives, giving you more energy and time to invest in things besides only handling all the stuff you have!

25. "You don't need even more room. You need less stuff."

~ Joshua Becker, The Even More of less

We usually seem like we need larger houses, bigger closets, bigger garages, etc. Much more frequently than not, our houses and the storage spaces in them are loaded with things we don't make use of, require, or even like!

For many of us, we do not need more space or a bigger house. We merely needless stuff!

Easy living quotes

I really hope these quotes on basic living will motivate you to declutter your home and organize your life, in the same way, they had paved the way for me!

10

QUESTIONS TO HELP YOU DECLUTTER MORE EFFECTIVELY

Decluttering your house is hard work, physically, emotionally and psychologically. Some products are very easy to decide what to do with it. However, it's not usually so clear. I've created a list of decluttering questions to ask yourself if you're struggling with decluttering, need to make clear for yourself if you must keep an item or get rid of it, or if you just want to make your decluttering go deeper and be extra efficient.

In some cases, it can help to have one more individual helping you declutter to ask the questions that can be tough to respond to. As soon as you address them, it ends up being clear what you must do with the item.

Nevertheless, sometimes we do not have somebody to help us; or we service decluttering in little pockets of time throughout the day, and it won't work to have someone help us. If that's the case, use this checklist of decluttering questions to help you declutter more effectively.

With some items, you will without struggle know what to do. The choices will certainly be simple and noticeable, and you likely will not need these decluttering questions

since you will address them without also thinking about it. This is usually the case for things you love and often use and know you want to maintain or things you have no need to keep and are happy to get rid of.

Every little thing you pick to keep in your house should have the ability to pass the test of each of these decluttering concerns. These questions help you determine if you actually use and/or enjoy a thing, and if the thing deserves the time/space/energy, it occupies in your life. That is an excellent indication you can get rid of it if a thing does not pass the test of these decluttering questions

When decluttering your house and deciding what to keep, these decluttering questions give you a range of things to think about; use them to shift your viewpoint, clarify and start thinking carefully about what you keep and why you're keeping it. As opposed to focusing on what to destroy, it can be practical to think about what to keep rather.

When decluttering, questions to ask

When you are decluttering your house and

having a hard time to determine if you ought to keep or get rid of a thing, the following questions give you some viewpoint and things to consider.

Both crucial decluttering questions

Every item in your home must be either something you use consistently or love. Begin with these 2 decluttering questions and make certain every little thing you decide to keep passes them certainly.

1. Do you use the product on a regular basis?

When was the last time you used it? Unless the thing is something you only use for a particular period or event; if you haven't used it in the last 6 months, you probably do not need it. If you cannot remember the last time you used it, let it go.

Your house needs only to hold things you use regularly. If there comes a period of time when you hardly ever use an item, you can find an appropriate option or borrow it from somebody else.

1. Do you desire this product?

Honestly asses your thing. Does it evoke positive or adverse feelings for you? Does it make you happy? If the emotion it raises for you is not a positive one, it does not deserve to be in your house. If it makes you really feel guilty, sad, insufficient, and so on, it probably isn't something you desire or need in your home.

Remember, your house should be your haven; only allow things that add value to your life to stay in your space. If it holds adverse feelings for you, don't allow yourself to be burdened by keeping it.

More Decluttering Questions

If you are still battling to decide what to do with a product after the two decluttering questions, take time to listen to decluttering questions to help you clear up the usefulness of each item and if it absolutely adds value to your life.

1. Do you have more than one of same item?

If you have more than of the same thing, or similar items, do you actually need all of them? Usually, one is enough.

1. If you really did not have this item, could you make use of another thing in its place?

Think of choices you can make use of if you did away with the item. Try to improvise single-use products and, rather, maintain things that can be used often or for a selection of objectives.

1. Do you have a hard time letting go of the item since you really feel guilty about losing money after you purchased it and no longer want or use it?

Feelings of shame can be difficult to let go of. Bear in mind, the money you used to purchase the item is currently invested. Hanging on to a product you aren't utilizing or loving won't get your refund.

If you aren't using or liking the item any longer, let it go. Use it as a lesson the next time you are shopping to be a lot more intentional about how you spend your money.

1. Was the item a gift, and you feel guilty about removing it?

Gifts are given to express love. The individual that offered you the present gave it to show their love for you.

Let it go if it's no longer something you like or make use of. It's your home, your space, your time, your life. You must be deliberate about what you permit into your home and just maintain the things you use on a regular basis or love.

To put it in point of view, imagine that you gave somebody a gift and after that found out they were only keeping it out of regret or because they really felt obliged to. You wouldn't wish to burden someone with a present you gave! Don't let yourself feel that way either.

1. Does the thing have a whole lot of sentimental value as it is hard to let go of?

I am not against keeping unique items that hold a great deal of emotional value for you. Nonetheless, you have to set some kind of limitations regarding the number of nostalgic items you intend to keep. The limitations will be various for every person. But setting limitations makes it much easier to be extra deliberate about what to keep.

Bear in mind that maintaining way too many special items reduces the relevance and significance of each thing, as they get overwhelmed and lost since there are only a lot of things. Yet selecting to keep only the very crucial, and the majority of special products, means you can highlight, and value them a lot more.

With this in mind, truthfully examine just how important or nostalgic a product is. If it's truly important to you, can you discover a means to repurpose, present, or use it in your home? If you don't intend to repurpose, use or present it, do you really need to keep it?

Taking a photo of a nostalgic thing is an excellent way to remember the thing and the memories it holds, without keeping the thing itself. While there are some items important enough to keep, frequently an image is enough.

1. Are you saving the thing "just in case"?

We often keep things "just in case," some unusual or unexpected scenarios happens in the future. First off, these scenarios hardly ever really happen and second of all, on the rare event, they do take place, we frequently either ignore the thing we were conserving "just in case" or find an alternative anyways.

Be reasonable regarding your "just in case" scenario. How likely is it to, in fact, happen? Moreover, if it did, could you find an alternate thing to make use of if you let go of this one?

1. Do you have plans to use the product "someday"?

Once more, be realistic about the likelihood of "someday" really happening. We frequently conserve things with the most effective intentions of getting around to them, yet never really get to it.

If you are convinced, you will use a thing "someday," offer on your own a firm time frame. Place it in your schedule. Let it go if the time limit arrives and you haven't made use of the item.

1. Is the thing making its keep in your house? Does the product add value to your life?

In order to stay in your room, a thing needs to add value to your life. Whatever we have needs our energy and time. We should purchase it, look after it, tidy it, maintain it, store it, etc. With this in mind, is this product adding adequate value to your life to make its keep?

1. Would certainly you get this item once again if you didn't already have it and saw it in a store?

Sometimes things remain unused and we continue to maintain them, whether or not we need or desire them. A fantastic way to test this is to ask on your own if you would buy it again if you were going shopping today. If you would hand over the purchase rate you paid for this item again, be honest with yourself and decide.

1. If you were moving, would you wish to pack, move, and unbox this thing?

This is an additional excellent test to help you determine only how much you value a thing. I like to visualize I'm transferring to a 3rd-floor walk-up apartment or condo. Ask yourself if the product is useful enough to you that you would certainly intend to lug it up to three trips of stairways.

1. Could somebody else gain from this item more than you?

If you're having a hard time to let go of something, this is a wonderful method to move your point of view. Rather than being in your house unused or seldom made use of, picture the value and benefit it might give someone else's life. Sometimes shifting our point of view to one of generosity makes it much easier to let go of items.

1. Does this item fit with your way of living and the season of life you're in TODAY?

Seasons of life, our rate of interests, and our requirements change over time. Also, if a thing was something we used or loved in 2015, that does not indicate we still use or like it today.

Just keep what you require, like, and use in your current way of life. Holding on to things from our previous way of life or season of life only adds clutter to our environment.

The exact same goes for saving things for the future. The products in our houses need to be things we use and enjoy today. Saving things for the future is a fast way to add a great deal of mess to our homes. Set sensible limitations about what you will save for future usage.

1. Just how would you really feel if this product was no longer in your home?

Envision; you removed the item. Exactly how would you feel? Would you be eliminated to no more need to manage it? Do you think you would certainly also remember it after a week of it being gone? Would you really feel depressing if you really did not see it daily?

Honestly, analyzing your feelings is a great way to set a thing's importance in your house.

1. Do you have a place for this product?

Every product you determine to keep must have a house that's logical and quickly accessible, making it easy to put it away. Things without a house commonly end up as a mess. If you do not have a place for this thing, find a place, make an environment or get rid of it!

1. Just how will you use this product and when?

Often reasonably specifying for ourselves

exactly how and when we will use an item makes it easier to determine only how most likely we are to, in fact, use it. If you cannot believe in a certain and realistic time or means you will certainly use the product in the near future, you possibly don't need to keep it.

1. Do you really feel obligated or expected to keep this item?

Your home needs to be your sanctuary, filled with only things that offer you and add value to your life. If you really feel required or expected to help an item you do not make use of or enjoy, it is unfair to you or your goal to declutter your home.

Inform them you are functioning to declutter your house and no longer want to help the thing if you feel pressure from someone else to help a thing. Allow them to know they are welcome to take the product; however, if they do not desire it, you will be doing away with it. When decluttering and reducing your house, setting firm limits for what you allow in your environment is crucial.

1. If the product needs fixing, exactly how and when will you repair it?

If you are genuinely willing to invest the energy, money, and/or time to repair the thing, ask yourself.

Do you have the required skills to do the fixing or will you need to work with somebody else?

Place a deadline to complete the repair in your calendar and adhere to it. If the due day passes hasn't been repaired, let it go. It will likely never get done if it still hasn't been repaired.

1. Exists a much better method you could make use of the space this product is using up?

In some cases, we help a product by default because we've constantly had it. If you are uncertain about maintaining a product, envision various other means you can use the room it occupies. Perhaps you might use its room for something you love that means a lot to you. Instead, possibly, you would only leave the space vacant and appreciate the white room you have actually produced.

Perk Tip

This list of decluttering concerns ought to provide you with some brand-new point of view and explanation for items you are battling to let go of.

11

STEPS TO DECLUTTER YOUR HOME

Before I began decluttering my home and accepting minimalism, I usually felt disappointed with the time and energy. I was spending enough time of my days managing our stuff. It is so releasing to declutter and let go of the excess things we owned and only keep what we like and use on a regular basis.

If you are ready to begin decluttering your house and life and change towards a simpler, minimalist life, right here are some ideas to help you begin. Taking the primary steps of decluttering is often the hardest. The idea of decluttering your entire house can really feel overwhelming to you at times.

Here are a few actions to start decluttering and help your energy to declutter your house and welcome minimalism:

Step 1: clear about your vision and likewise, also your "why."

Why do you intend to declutter your space and begin living a minimalist life? Get clear on your own about why you are doing this. What matters the most to you? What do you intend to get by living much merely and minimally? Ask on your own only how your space is currently making you feel? Just how do you want to feel in your house?

What's your vision?

Decluttering your life takes a lot of difficult physical, mental, and psychological jobs. Letting go of your stuff is tough mentally and psychologically. When you're battling to declutter and accept minimalism, it helps to have a clear vision of why you're putting in all this work.

What do you want minimalism to look like for you?

Exactly how will you define when the amount of things is enough for you? What do you want minimalism to look like for you? Minimalism is a way of living that will advance and change as the season of life you're in adjustments.

Be clear about your vision for how minimalism and simple living will look in your life. Clarify why you are placing your time and energy right into decluttering and re-organizing your home.

Step 2: Make a strategy; however, do not fail to remember to take action.

Developing a program for only how you wish to resolve to declutter your space is essential. Having a plan to comply with makes it simpler to dive in and get to function, rather than fretting about what to do and when to do it. If you'll declutter space by space or declutter all like things at one time, determine.

What will you make with the stuff you're doing away with?

Identify what you wish to make with the right stuff you're getting rid of. What will you do with the garbage/recycling? Decide where you will contribute some of those things. Figure out where you will offer it if you want to market anything. I also advise giving yourself a target date to get it as a timeframe to donate any item that wasn't sold.

Offering the right stuff for decluttering can be an excellent way to make some additional money. But it can likewise slow down and impede your progress. Marketing items takes a great deal of time (taking images, uploading to buy, referring purchasers, setting up meet-ups, making up individuals that don't appear, etc.). Hanging on to things while you're waiting to offer indicates your room isn't gotten rid of as promptly, and there's constantly the risk of altering your mind or the "sell" stack being returned into your home (specifically with tiny children around!). A garage sale is an additional alternative, simply ensure you set a firm date for sale. It makes sure that it occurs in fact. It also devotes you to give away anything that does not sell after the yard sale.

When will you declutter?

When will you declutter, make a decision? Make time for it, put it in your schedule and prioritize it. I recommend adding it to your schedule and treating it like any type of other appointment. If you do not set the details chunks of time aside to work with decluttering, it may get avoided. Determine what works best for you and your timetable. In some cases, it will be setting up 15 mins a day, setting aside 3 hours on the weekend or somewhere in between. Figure out what benefits you, schedule it and hold on to your own responsibility to follow up.

Focus on the spaces to declutter.

Figure out what creates the most stress and anxiety. Make those locations' concerns. Make a listing of all the rooms or types of stuff in your home and rate them from the highest possible to cheapest decluttering top priority.

Do not forget to act!

Keep in mind that a strategy is only efficient if you actually do the work and place the plan into activity. Make your unique strategy, bind it with perfect calculations and fit it with your own potentials and realities. Give it equal importance, never dare to hesitate with it. In fact, BEGIN decluttering right today!

Step 3: Do a quick sweep via the entire house

When I began decluttering, this is just how I started. I went and took a box through the entire home rapidly getting rid of anything I might see that we really did not love or use. It was impressive how much stuff I gathered swiftly. I had so many things remaining that I had no attachment to and recognized I didn't even care if they remained in our house! Much of the things were decorative things that were simply filling the space, but served no function and held no emotional value.

It removes a layer of surface area mess and doesn't need you to make any kind of challenging or emotional choices. You can alter your way of living and take control of your things!

Step 4: Clear your surface areas and work on keeping them clear

Make a spot for mail, papers, billing cords, keys, publications magazines, periodicals, and anything else that you often find cluttering up your surfaces. When you've made space for these things, work towards keeping your brand-new routine of putting things away in their new places.

Keeping these surfaces clear will immediately make your room appear less cluttered and more beautiful. This big aesthetic effect will urge and encourage you to keep going.

Tip 5: Declutter somewhere simple

You intend to keep your momentum and continue to have successes to get self-confidence and motivate you to continue towards minimalism. Find somewhere easy and relatively fast to declutter; an area that is not excessively nostalgic or too much work. Begin small, don't handle a whole space. Instead, tackle a smaller location like one drawer, one rack, or one area of space. Great locations to attempt are the shower room, the cupboard, the coat wardrobe, or a few kitchen area cabinets. Resolve the room. Then celebrate one more decluttering success under your belt!

Step 6: Next go on to the area that is your greatest concern

Symphonious 2, you determined the area that causes you the most anxiety and made it a top priority. Carry on to that area next. Tackling this location will provide you the largest influence on your life.

If the playthings and play location create you the most stress and take up most of your time choosing and maintaining, start your mark of decluttering from right there. Possibly it's the space you spend one of the most times in every day.

Ruthlessly decluttering this area will certainly produce even more time for you and space in your home. It will have a big positive effect on your life and the benefits of your work decluttering will certainly be rigid. Absolutely nothing encourages you decluttering and reducing like having a substantial source of your tension eliminated and seeing the positive outcomes right away!

Step 7: Follow your strategy and resolve your whole house.

Since you've had success decluttering the area of your house that produces you the most stress and anxiety and keep following your plan to overcome the remainder of your home. Work from best to the majority of cost-effective worry. Continue to devote and set up a time to decluttering. Make your decluttering work a top priority in your timetable. Hold yourself answerable to it and follow up.

You've had many successes by this point; make use of those to inspire yourself to keep putting in the time and initiative. Taking before and after photos of your space can be a wonderful means to keep an eye on your effort, particularly if you're gradually re-organizing your home. One more good incentive is to track the number of things you've eliminated. Keeping a tally reveals that you're making development also if you really feel prevented or uninspired to continue.

Commemorate your success as you keep working in the direction of a clutter-free and very little home! Beginning to discover exactly how your recently decluttered rooms make you feel. Do you feel calmer? Less stressed? Are you delighted to entertain over? Are you spending less time cleaning and grabbing?

12

EASY THINGS TO GET RID OF

When you're initially starting to declutter your house, it can feel overwhelming. Sometimes it's hard even to know where to start! Whether you want to declutter your house promptly, or preparing to overcome your house gradually as time permits, beginning to declutter can feel like a significant task to tackle. The truth is, it is a great deal of work to declutter years of ownerships and "stuff." The good information is it does not have to be overwhelming! Below is a list of 30 very easy things to remove to kick-start your decluttering efforts and make progress decluttering your home.

The very first step can be the hardest action

By that I suggest, taking action and, in fact, starting to declutter can be the hardest component.

Usually, when you get going, you get in a decluttering groove and it's much easier to keep going. Use this checklist as a method to kick-start your decluttering efforts to proceed or start decluttering.

By letting go of things you neither use neither love and welcoming life with less, you start developing time, freedom, and space so you can appreciate people and activities that matter most to you as opposed to spending

most of your energy and time managing the "things" in your house.

Kick-start your decluttering energy

Even if you've been decluttering for some time, we can all shed our energy or inspiration at times. This list can also be a great way to kick-start your decluttering again, get your decluttering groove back and keep working in the direction of your objective of a simplified house and life.

If you have a hard time to begin or continue with your decluttering initiatives, you need something, to begin with, build your momentum, get the motivation and confidence to keep it working. In times like these, it's best to deal with something easy and fast to declutter.

Starting with an area that's going to be a great deal of work or full of nostalgic items will likely add in your feelings of confusion. Decluttering things that are simple to allow go of and quick to declutter will enable you to make progression rapidly. You'll kick-start your decluttering efforts with these very easy to allow go of items.

30 simple things to do away with

If you are really feeling overwhelmed, having a tough time starting, or perhaps you don't also recognize where to begin, this list is for you! Below are 30 fast and very easy things to declutter from your house to kick-start your decluttering and minimalism trip. You'll construct your self-confidence and inspiration to take on the harder locations when you've made some development decluttering these simple items.

Getting rid of things, no matter how small or apparent they seem, can frequently kick-start your decluttering and encourage you to help get rid of things. Helping you take the first action and beginning to declutter!

Kitchen

1. Plastic containers

Do away with any plastic containers that don't have a lid or ones that are warped or damaged.

2. Papers and pictures on your fridge

A messy refrigerator can gradually turn the entire kitchen really unkempt and messy. Remove anything out of date or otherwise important. Attempt cleaning off your refrigerator completely and see how it changes the feeling of your kitchen area!

3. Fridge magnets

The less you continue your refrigerator, the fewer magnets you'll need, and the fewer magnets you have, the less you'll be able to hold on to your refrigerator, developing less visual clutter in your kitchen area. Win-win!

4. Expired food in your pantry

It can be shocking the number of old things that can be lurking in the rear of the kitchen! You can also get rid of any kind of things that aren't expired, but you know your family members will likely never consume and take them to your local food bank.

5. Any kitchen area gadget you have not used since 2015

If you did not use it in 2014, you possibly will never ever use it. Definitely get rid of it if you do not even know what it is!

6. Little devices you have not made use of in the last year

Same as # 5, if you haven't used it in the past year, you most likely don't need it!

7. Mugs you never use

Instead of leaving the mugs you never make use of at the back of the cupboard, just get rid of them! If you never choose it for your coffee or tea, no need to allow it to occupy valuable cabinet room!

8. Tea towels and dishcloths you never make use of

If you have so many tea towels and dishcloths that you never get to the ones at the back of the cabinet or cupboard before you replenish them with freshly cleaned ones, remove the bonus. Think of the number you need for your family members and remove the extras!

Washroom

9. Cosmetics you haven't used in the last 6 months or have expired.

Also, though it seems tiny and insignificant, getting rid of makeup you never ever wear is an outstanding decluttering exercise. It helps get you in the way of thinking of only maintaining what you enjoy and use, and getting rid of the rest!

10. Fifty percent of shampoo, conditioner, lotion, etc.

If you got something new to try, used it for a while, and decided you really did not like it, do away with it! There is no point in keeping half-used bottles you know you do not intend to keep using.

11. Excess or duplicate bathroom playthings

Many children are perfectly pleased with a couple of mugs or containers from the cooking area to play with during bath time. Do away with anything that seldom obtains played with and any kind of matches. Toys that squirt water can promptly end up being musty on the inside, so do away with any mold and mildew inside.

12. Expired medicine

Take a glance through your medicine stash for anything expired and do away with it. A lot of pharmacies take expired or no longer required drugs and properly deal with them.

13. Towels you never make use of.

I have two towels. One is enough for our family members, plus a few visitor towels. Get rid of them if you have towels that you never ever use because you have favorites or so many that you never ever get to the base of the stack!

Living environment

14. Publications you have actually read and will certainly never ever check out again

Usually, we read books once and do not review them again. Donate books you have already checked out to your public library. After that, you can constantly borrow them if you change your mind and wish to review them again.

15. DVDs you have actually watched and will never ever view once more.

Once again, be honest with yourself if you are truly most likely to watch a DVD once more. Give away DVDs to your public library and borrow them if you ever want to watch them once more.

16. Old magazines

Read the magazine, and recycle it. Hanging on to old publications can swiftly add clutter to your home. And more often than not, they are never looked at again.

17. Brochures

The less lure to acquire more things while you're decluttering, the better! Get rid of brochures and remove the temptation to buy.

18. Additional toss pillows that constantly wind up on the floor

Make a decision just how many throw pillows you actually use on your couch or chairs. Your living room will promptly look tidier without the unused bonuses.

Bedrooms/Closets

19. Single socks without a suit or holey socks

This is quite noticeable. If it's broken or doesn't have a match, eliminate it!

20. Footwear that injures your feet

I think all of us (particularly females) have shoes that harm our feet. But we hang on because of the fact that we spent a great deal of money on them or keep "simply in instance." If they are not comfortable, you possibly never ever, or extremely seldom, wear them get rid of them!

21. Undergarments with openings in them.

One more evident one! It's time to claim

goodbye if your undergarments have holes where there should not be openings!

22. Sheet sets you never use

I discovered 2 sets of sheets per bed are enough; one to wash, one to redo the bed with. Keep your favorite 1 or 2 sets, and get rid of the rest.
Toys/Playroom

23. Children's books.

Your children have actually outgrown or do not use such books.

If your children have books they have actually outgrown, you don't delight in checking out or do not like the content/language, get rid of them! There are many great kids' books. You don't need to hold on to publications you don't enjoy reading with your children or are no longer age proper.

24. Duplicate playthings

Try to find anything your children have multiples of, do they truly need them all? If you have 10 rounds of various sizes, get rid of some in moderate sizes.

25. Toys your children have outgrown are damaged or missing items

A fast method to start decluttering the playthings is to cut down anything grown out of, damaged, missing out on items, or merely not played with. Make a quick move through the toys and eliminate the very easy playthings to allow go of.

Miscellaneous

26. Charging cables, you don't understand what they're for

Get rid of it if you don't recognize what it charges! Many devices use the exact same kind of charging cord, so choose the number of a certain type you need and get rid of the rest.

27. Anything you don't like or even respect

Take a fast go through your home and do away with style products you do not enjoy and/or don't have unique meaning to you. Usually, we buy decor items to fill up the environment, yet they simply end up including mess to our homes and hold no significance for us. Having fewer style items lets you highlight those products so that you can enjoy them even more!

28. Cleaning up products you never ever make use of

If you got a brand-new item to attempt, yet don't like it, do away with it. There's no point in allowing products you will not use to take up room in your home.

29. Old paint canisters

Get rid of them if you have paint canisters in your garage in shades that aren't even in your house anymore. Take old paint to your neighborhood paint recycling center.

30. Pens that do not work or you do not like the means they write

Certainly, do away with any type of pens that do not function. Additionally, get rid of any type of that you don't like utilizing. There's no point allowing things to remain in your house you don't desire or make use of.

Kick-start your decluttering!

Working through this listing will help you discover things that are very easy and quick to declutter. A lot of us don't feel excessively connected to our pens or charging cords! Use this list to kick-start your decluttering and dive in, particularly if you do not know where to start or are really feeling overwhelmed.

As I claimed before, in some cases taking the primary step can be the hardest. Normally, as soon as you begin decluttering, you'll get the motivation, self-confidence, and energy to help to declutter. Remember, you do not need to declutter your whole home in a day. Keep working and keep your objective of an organized home that provides you even more time, space, and liberty in mind.

13
EASY PRACTICES TO MAINTAIN A CLUTTER-FREE HOUSE

If you merely have many things, it's difficult to preserve a clutter-free house. A lot less and arranged or functional house.

As vital as decluttering is, it's not the only vital method to Organize your house and life. Setting day-to-day practices and regimens to help a clutter-free home are similarly crucial for clearing the clutter, to begin with.

If you don't have solid routines and practices to keep your house clutter-free progressing, you'll likely wind up exactly where you were with a cluttered house that's tough to take care of.

less stuff + a couple of basic habits & regimens make it easy to keep a clutter-free house!

Even when you have less stuff, your house will certainly still get unpleasant sometimes. You and your family members still live there and use your house!

Yet when you have less stuff, incorporated with regimens and habits to keep a clutter-free house, your house will be a lot easier to manage.

Not only that, keeping your home tidy will certainly take less time and effort. Giving you even more time to live and appreciate your life, not simply clean up after it!

Easy Practices & daily routine-works to remove the clutter and help your home tidy.

Today I want to share 12 very easy regimens and practices to help you keep a clutter-free house now and in the future!

These behaviors and regimens will certainly not only help you as you are in the process of decluttering and eliminating the excess things from your house. They will also help you keep your home clutter-free relocating ahead.

12 easy and fast routines to maintain a clutter-free house.

1. An area for everything and anything in its place

One of the very best ways to preserve a clutter-free home is having a place for every product in your house, and entering into the practice of placing every little thing away in its location on a regular basis.

Clutter is typically the result of products that either doesn't have a home or you don't know what to do with. When something doesn't have a house, it often sits out, jumbling your surface areas and your home.

But when everything has an assigned location to keep it, it makes it much easier to help a clutter-free house.

If a product does not have a home or you cannot find a good place to keep it, either do some decluttering till you can find a home for it. Or ask yourself if the thing truly needs to remain in your house.

Don't put it down, put it away

As soon as you have a house for everything, the following component of this behavior is actually placing things away when you're done using them.

The more you enter the practice of putting things away, the less will certainly be omitted throughout your house, triggering clutter.

I like to remind myself of the "one-touch rule," which suggests you aim to touch things once.

Rather than placing something down to manage later (typically leaving you with a lot of clutter, or a huge heap of things to manage at the end of the day) simply try putting them in an organized format every time.

Another way to keep in mind it is this: don't place things down, put them away!

Naturally, you tend to get active, or life takes place and things will not constantly get put away right away. The more you get in the routine of placing things away in their home after you're done using them, the much easier it will certainly be to keep your house clutter-free and clean.

2. Notification of the common causes of mess and make a plan for those items

Typically, the very same couple of sorts of things

are the largest sources of clutter in a house. Perhaps it's garments, paperwork, playthings, dishes, keys/phones/wallets, and so on.

As you set about your day, observe the typical sources of clutter and the remaining stuff on your surfaces and around your home.

Firstly, start decluttering and organizing those groups of things, when you understand your most typical sources of clutter. When you have less, it makes keeping up with and managing the stuff so much easier.

Then, make a strategy to deal with the common causes of mess. find or make houses for all the items that generally create clutter around your home.

See to it their houses are rational, ideally maintaining things near where you use them.

And see to it their homes are conveniently obtainable. If it takes excessive work to place something away, it likely will not get do away with it.

Make it simple to keep things in their environment!

3. Have a system to keep documents from piling up

Documents seem to be among the most usual reasons for mess for many of us. Much so that I assume, it's value taking the time to set up a system to handle paperwork, especially.

Not to point out, the level surface environments in our homes appear to be magnets for the paper mess. It's easy to set one thing down to deal with, later on. However, due to the fact that mess brings in clutter before you know it, you have a whole heap!

The very best means to help paper clutter from accumulating is to has a great system in a position to take care of it before it has a chance to accumulate. To be effective, your paper management system needs to be quick to make use of and simple to maintain.

My preferred means to deal with documentation is utilizing a command. It doesn't need to be elaborate or fancy. In fact, the less complex, the better!

Set up a command facility to deal with your lifestyle and habits. Instead of going down documentation on any type of available surface in your house, you can put it away quite easily. Find it when you need it and avoid the dreadful piles of paper mess!

4. Have a continuous contribution box within reach at all times.

One more straightforward, yet amazing means to make it simple to preserve a clutter-free house is by keeping a contribution box useful and offered at all times.

Throughout the day, when you encounter something you no longer make use of, need, or like, simply add it to your contribution box. (Or naturally, toss it out right then if it's trash or not worth giving away!). When your contribution box is complete, drop the stuff off at your contribution facility and begin again!

A continuous contribution box makes it easy to declutter as you tackle your day. Instead of waiting on designated "decluttering times," by which time you might have forgotten what you intended to get rid of, a handy contribution box makes decluttering on the move easy.

The fewer barriers you have to declutter the simpler it will certainly be to clear the clutter and help your house clutter-free and neat!

5. Declutter as you go about your day.

Decluttering as you tackle your day is an outstanding practice to get involved in to help preserve a clutter-free house.

Like I said above, whenever you encounter something you no more use, desire, or require, add it to your donation box or toss it out right after that.

If you get in the routine of doing this consistently, you'll make great progress in the direction of clearing the clutter from your home and also keeping your house clean and clutter-free.

After all, is said and done, decluttering isn't something you do. Our needs alter, our preferences change, the season of life we remain in adjustments. and also, a lot more you declutter and see the benefits of dealing with less, the more eager and fired up you end up being to allow go of even more.

Make eliminating things you don't use, enjoy, or need part of your daily routine, and also, you'll reach your decluttering objectives also faster!

6. Do a quick every day reset of your house

Getting in the practice of placing things away as quickly as you're done using them is a great behavior to enter to keep your home clutter-free. However, occasionally life occurs, and it does not always get done!

My favorite way to stay on top of keeping your house clutter-free and neat, also on busy days, is doing a fast day-to-day reset of our home.

A reset isn't a deep clean and shouldn't take long. Instead, it's a quick tidy to put things away and reset your house.

Getting in the habit of costs 10 minutes a day grabbing, placing things away, and usually tidying your home will certainly go a long method towards keeping a clutter-free home.

And the most effective part is, once you are in the behavior of doing a quick reset on a daily basis, it won't take much time or effort. When you stay on top of any kind of messes by tidying up at the very least daily, things do not have a chance to pile up or get out of control.

Pick a time of day that works best for your routine and purpose to do your reset daily.

I like to do a fast reset every night before the children go to bed. It's so great to wake up each morning to a clean house, rather than the previous day's mess!

7. Clear the flat surface areas consistently

As you're doing your day-to-day reset (or getting in the behavior of putting things away when you're finished with them), removing your level surface environments is an especially important part to keep in mind.

Level surfaces, like kitchen environment counters, coffee tables, kitchen tables, nightstands, etc. appear to be magnets for clutter. Once more, the much more frequently you stay on top of clearing off these surfaces, the easier it will be to keep them clear.

Do not give piles a chance to create!

Rather, enter the practice of erasing the flat surface areas at the very least once daily to help preserve a clutter-free and clean house.

8. Make your bed

Making your bed may not seem that significant. It remains in your bedroom, and few individuals most likely see that area anyhow, why does it matter?

It's more about moving your attitude than anything else and enabling you to start your day with a sense of success and initiative.

Making your bed only takes a couple of minutes; however, instantly changes the way your bedroom feels and looks. It makes the whole area look tidier, cleaner, and much more welcoming.

This small practice can have a domino effect that helps motivate various other little practices to keep your house tidy

For example, since your room looks so wonderful with the bed made, you might be influenced to put your dirty clothes in the interfere instead of on the flooring.

Due to the fact that you saw the distinction one small activity made to your bedroom, or it might motivate you to place your unclean dishes in the dishwashing machine rather of by the sink.

Not only can it motivate you to help your house

be tidier, but also a nicely made bed is such a wonderful treat to return to at the end of a tiring day.

9. Keep your kitchen tidy.

The kitchen environment often tends to be the heart of the house. It's typically where we gather and hang out with family and friends. Due to the fact that it's such a hardworking, well-used space, getting in the practice of maintaining your cooking environment clean and clutter-free will certainly impact the feel of the entire home.

There are numerous simple methods to get in the practice of keeping your cooking environment tidy. You can attempt cleaning as you cook, rapidly tidying up after each dish, recycling the very same drinking glass throughout the day, etc. Even meal planning can help food from creating clutter in your kitchen.

For even more habits to help keep your kitchen area clutter-free, take a look at this message for plenty of ideas!

10. Use the "one in, one out" rule

While getting rid of the clutter is a fundamental part of a clutter-free house, stopping the inflow of new things from entering your house is equally vital.

First, deal with making even more deliberate buying choices, so you aren't getting things you don't really need or will not use.

You can also practice treating on your own to things that won't trigger mess when you seem like purchasing but do not wish to add even more "things" to your house.

After that, when you do bring or buy something brand-new right into your house. Try to balance it by adhering to the "one in, one out" rule. Get rid of something else to make room when you bring something new right into your house.

Try getting rid of two or three or even more things for each new product you bring in if you desire to kick it up a notch!

11. Completely reset your house at the beginning of the week

Along with doing daily resets in your house, a much deeper once-a-week reset can be a fantastic behavior to help maintain a clutter-free house.

I like to do our once-a-week reset on Sunday evenings to begin the week off with a clean house ready to take on the week in advance.

The weekly reset is essentially like an everyday reset, only a little bit deeper. Along with getting and putting things away, I also like to:

- Dish prepare for the week

- Get groceries

- Clean our freezer, refrigerator, and cupboard

- Do a little food preparation for the week

- Collect the trash and take it out

- Capture upon any kind of washing

It feels fantastic to begin the week feeling in addition to things instead of currently really feeling behind.

12. Own fewer things!

And of course, one truly important habit to

preserve a clutter-free house is simply possessing less stuff!

Cleaning the mess from your house is extremely important to keep your house clutter-free, arranged, and useful. Not only will all the practices and routines in this book be a great deal more difficult if you have much stuff to start with. Your house will certainly be truly tough to preserve in general.

The mix of possessing less paired with setting some behaviors to help it tidy and clutter-free is the trick to creating a streamlined house that is very easy to keep, satisfying to be in, and less demanding to manage.

Progress, not perfection

Aim to add one or two brand-new behaviors at a time. Once you feel like you've grasped those routine works for a few days add in one or two or even more and bear in mind, it's more crucial to aim for development, not excellence. Do not beat yourself up if you miss out on a few days. Beginning where you are, get back on course and help to move on!

14
BENEFIT OF SIMPLIFYING AND DECLUTTERING

Simplifying and decluttering our house and our lives have allowed me to accomplish all that, and so much more!

Cleaning up and preserving a neat home is less complicated if you have lesser stuff! There are fewer "things" to pick up and tidy around, as there are fewer things themselves to clean!

But the influence of simplifying our home and lives has actually gone far past that. When I first set out to clear the clutter, today I desire to share 11 advantages of simplifying that I wasn't expecting. And these advantages have actually been such a welcome surprise!

If you're ready to organize and declutter your house and are trying to find an extra dosage of inspiration to improve your motivation, look into these 11 shocking benefits of simplifying, you might not be anticipating any of them!

11 Unanticipated benefits of decluttering and organizing

1. Better in your house

Feeling material and satisfied in your house is an awesome advantage of decluttering and organizing.

You not only get more space in your house when you get rid of the clutter from your home. But you also produce even more satisfaction and gratefulness for the home you currently have.

Possibly, you don't need a larger house or more storage space; you simply need less stuff loaded in it!

Not only that but when your home isn't filled with "things" that need your time, space, and energy, your house really feels less stressful and becomes less of a time suck. You can clean, tidy, and keep your house a lot less complicated, and when each thing you choose to help conveniently has a designated space actually to keep it, it's simple to use it, put it away, and find it once again when you need it!

2. Better relationships

I had not been expecting decluttering to have such a huge impact on my connections, yet it has been a massive unforeseen benefit of organizing!

When your house and your "stuff" occupy less of your time and energy, you have more energy and time to buy your partnerships with the people you love!

You can offer your family and friends more of your time, interest, energy, and emphasis. In a sense, each of these things is now feasible to you as your house and your "things" do not take so much of it. And when you can invest your time and energy right into your relationships with individuals you love most, those partnerships can thrive and grow much deeper!

Not only that, but when your home is less complicated and kept clean, you are most likely to feel less tense and less animosity towards your family members. It's because you no longer seem like you're coping with an endless order of business or disorderly mess. And getting rid of a resource of lingering stress and anxiety or resentment is an excellent means to produce the possibility to boost your partnerships with your family.

3. Extra joy & perseverance

One of the most unexpected benefits of simplifying our home was the enhancement it made to my state of mind. I really did not understand only how stressed out all the "things" in our house, made me up until it was gone.

When our house was jumbled, disorderly, and untidy, it made me feel overwhelmed and irritable. My patience would be brief since I already really felt bewildered by how much time and energy our home and "things" took from me. I need order in our house to really feel serene and calm.

Getting rid of all the right stuff we didn't use or need was such a straightforward remedy to this problem.

Even now, if I ever before begin to feel grouchy or stressed out cleaning up and taking care of the house, that's normally an indicator that it's time to do an additional quick round of decluttering.

4. Less anxiousness

Research has revealed that a cluttered atmosphere can create stress and anxiety in individuals.

Not only can the clutter overstimulate your mind, causing stress and anxiety and making it hard to unwind. Additionally, the looming thoughts of all you need to do to cleanse up, find things, take care of your home, and so on can trigger a lot of tension and stress, and anxiety.

When your house is jumbled, disordered and out of order, life, as a whole, can really feel out of control, resulting in anxiety and anxiousness. By decluttering and organizing, we can drop a substantial source of stress from our lives and homes, and lower our anxiety degree also.

Eliminating the clutter from your home can even help improve your rest! A clutter-free bedroom provides your mind an opportunity to remainder, kick back, and sleep far better.

5. Even more money & economic freedom

When you choose to organize and declutter, you

have made the selection to have less and when you pick to have less, you generally tend to acquire less. Not only can this save you money, yet it can also give you much more financial flexibility.

Your spending behaviors enhance as you end up being more thoughtful and willful about your acquisitions. You usually tend to buy less generally as you begin to understand you already have enough!

As you become much more willful with your spending practices, it offers you the flexibility to spend your money on what is very important to you.

6. Less purchasing

As an extension of conserving your money, an unforeseen advantage of simplifying are the determinants of why you have a tendency to shop less.

How much time do you invest in running duties: checking out things to purchase, thinking about the price, investigating the importance of the things you're planning to purchase, so on!

When you choose to own less, you pick to purchase less. and this frees up a lot of time and energy formerly eaten by taking in and getting more "things"!

Rather, you can pick to use this time and energy for something that will certainly offer you a better long-lasting incentive. Like going after leisure activity, you love or spending quality time with the people you like.

All without filling your house with the mess that

you'll need to tidy, organize, pick up, seek, take care of, etc. later!

7. Even more flexibility & opportunities for fun

When you invest less time managing all the "stuff" you own, you give yourself more flexibility and possibilities to have fun!

You can say yes much more, knowing you will not support on family duties or pay for it later because your home will be out of control since your house will not take up so a lot of your time any longer when there is less stuff, only.

"less things = less mess. less mess = more time.

Even more time = freedom."

~ through Janine Young

8. A lot more self-confidence

When your home remains in order in such a way that makes you feel comfortable, happy, and pleased, your self-confidence can boost. You really feel in control of your house, not vice versa. It gives you a feeling of achievement that makes you feel excellent and boosts your self-confidence.

Selecting to live with less can sometimes really feel counter-cultural in our consumer-driven society.

Understanding the advantages of organizing makes you feel happier and healthier; you really feel certain in your selection to simplify your house.

When you declutter and simplify, you could also feel even more excitement to host pals and family in your house. When you feel delighted and certain with your home, not embarrassed by the mess anymore, you may be more likely to welcome people into your house, which only helps to proceed to grow your relationships!

9. More life in your life

When you organize and declutter your home and life, you have a tendency to end up being extra conscious of where your time and interest are going. You are much better able to make deliberate selections if your time and interest are going where you want them to.

This mindfulness permits you to be a lot more alive in your days, as opposed to getting distracted by your "stuff" and the time and energy it takes up.

Also, decluttering and simplifying enable you to live for today, as opposed to living in the past or fretting about the future.

Rather than keeping things "only in situation," you might need them "one day," decluttering helps you to stop stressing about every possible future scenario and emphasis on what you use and need right now, in the alive.

Maintaining some sentimental items from the past behaves. However, many sentimental things suggest they go from special, important items to a pile of clutter instead. It's tough to live in today when your space is cluttered with the past.

Decluttering and simplifying your house help once; you release concerns and fears about the future, in addition, to releases you from living in the past. All so you are totally free to take pleasure in the here and now moment and who you are today!

10. Start valuing experiences over "things."

Another surprising advantage of simplifying is the means it shifts your general attitude to concentrate on what you can do, not what you can get.

You start to recognize that all the "stuff" you acquire, will ultimately come to be the stuff you invest your energy and time in cleaning, arranging, seeking, grabbing, etc.

Rather, experiences let you make memories, have a good time, and so on, all without including any more "stuff" to your house and life to take care of or create a mess.

11. More thankfulness.

Of all the unexpected advantages of simplifying, this has to be one of the most impactful ones.

You have even more time and energy to value and appreciate what you do have when you have fewer things.

Since it adds value to your life, you acknowledge that what you have is sufficient. Since you enjoy and use what you possess, it's easier now to value what you have when it's valuable to you as opposed to being a burden taking up more energy and time than it deserves.

Not only that yet as your attitude shifts from wanting to build up more and more, but you also begin to discover and feel thankful for what you currently have.

12. Un-anticipated benefits of simplifying

I hope these 11 unanticipated benefits of simplifying inspire you to see that decluttering and simplifying have to do with a lot more.

Don't get me wrong, that's a fantastic benefit of simplifying in itself but the advantages of organizing your house and your life can go a lot deeper than that. From your bank account to your state of mind and outlook on life, decluttering and simplifying can have an effect on your entire life!

If you're willing to let go of the mess, the excess, and the interruptions, there are so many advantages waiting on you!

AFTERWORD

A minimalist living is something you should have found out about a whole lot lately. Do you believe it is about doing away with every one of your possessions and simply enduring on the bare minimum? I need to say, you have actually obtained it all incorrectly.

In truth, minimalism is not about doing away with whatever and living with nothing; in fact, it is about decluttering your home and enduring with what you require. The rationale of a minimal way of life is not to be attached to products, have more room at your house, and have a hassle-free life.

Living a minimalist way of life is eliminating things that are unnecessary and do not actually offer a function in your life. Minimal living cannot be the same for everybody.

In a basic definition, minimalism is:

- To determine what is beneficial and important to you, and to do away with things that are not needed or do not add value to your life.

A good practice is to sit in your home and make a checklist of things you require. Adhere to your shopping list when you see a shop. Prevent any inconsistency.

A minimal way of life varies from one individual to another, but it focuses on the exact same core values, "LESS IS EVEN MORE."

HYGGE

The Danish Art of a Happy and Cozy Life

By
Edison Montgomery

Copyright © 2021

All Rights Reserved. This book or any portion thereof may not be reproduced or used in any manner whatsoever without the express written permission of the publisher except for the use of brief quotations in a book review.

ABSTRACT

Why you should consider this book

Hygge is a lot more of a prominent lifestyle trend that features cozy indoor style or "homemade" crafts and recipes. Hygge living is a method of life that needs slowing down and becoming more conscious of what is going on in the present minute.

In other terms, hygge denotes a quality of using simpler things using simpler means of any kind ranging from lighting beautiful candles in the evening to wearing sober clothing; and through all these simple means, hygge can make a person feel content and comfortable.

It's an art that can be exercised at anytime from anywhere, whether indoor or outdoor with your family members or just by yourself. Hygge is all about paving the way for a happy lifestyle for everyone from everywhere.

The art of Hygge mainly incorporates the act of acknowledging a sensation or moment as being relaxing or different in routes taken.

This book will, therefore, show you the best way to live a hygge lifestyle, leading to a happy life; thereby providing you the right guardian to overcome all anxious and depressing situations and consequently improving your overall well-being.

INTRODUCTION TO HYGGE

In the last couple of years and months, I am certain that you have encountered this particular word: Hygge, and you might have just assumed or wondered what it could mean exactly. Well, this is a chance to understand the term in detail and know how it is going to be useful to you.

Looking at the term "hoo-ga," it is a Danish idea that cannot be translated to one single word but yet incorporates a feeling of cozy satisfaction and well-being through delighting in the easy points in life.

Have you ever been delighted while reading a book at your home on a cool Sunday with just a cup of hot cocoa while snow is falling? Well, you have experienced Hygge. It's all about that particular feeling of satisfaction where you appreciate the present.

Hygge is such a vital part of being Danish that it

is considered "a specifying feature of our social identification and an indispensable area of Denmark national people," the happiness research institute CEO said this;

Meik Wiking "In other words, what liberty is to Americans ... hygge is to Danish people," Wiking says this in his publication of The Little Book of Hygge.

Denmark's nationwide coziness obsession is the main thing that put them on top of the world's happiest nation list, regardless of their infamously unpleasant winters. And recently, the remainder of the world has started to catch on to this remarkable way of life.

According to the 2016 World Happiness Report, Denmark clocked in as the world's happiest country. Wiking thought that favorable statistics could be credited to hygge. "The Danish people are exceptionally proficient at decoupling riches and wellness," he stated. "We concentrate on the small things that truly matter, consisting of investing our quality time with our families and friends and delighting in the good ideas in life."

That might be why the idea of hygge has experienced such popularity below in the United States. It appears like wherever you go, there will be someone who wants to understand how to master the art of hygge ideally.

Hygge (or to be "hyggeligt") does not need

learning "just how to," it is also embracing it as a way of life to acquire just about anything.

THE HISTORY OF HYGGE, WHAT IT ENTAILS, AND WHY YOU SHOULD CONSIDER HYGGE

Basically, Hygge requires your consciousness, a certain sluggishness, and the capacity not merely to exist. It is about identifying existing opportunities and enjoying the present. That is why so many individuals take 'hygge' down to being a 'sensation' because if you don't feel hygge, you are most likely not making use of the word. Hygge is about coziness and bordering yourself with the essential things like laughter, friendship, safety, security, and even more concrete things like warmth, light, seasonal food, and drinks that make life good.

Another meaning of hygge is "an art of developing affection," either on your own, with close friends, and family members within your residence.

While there's no one English word or easy definition to explain hygge, several can be used reciprocally to explain the concept of hygge, such as coziness, beauty, happiness, 'contentment,' security, knowledge, convenience, confidence, kinship, and simpleness.

It is an idea that approximately calls for a sensation of convenience and contentment, and indulges all the advantages and people in your life. It is connected to the concept that the Danish people are the happiest people on the planet. Hygge has been identified as the secret behind happiness.

Danish people developed hygge intending to make it through dullness, chilly, dark, and sameness. Hygge was identified as an undefinable sensation and a way for them to discover moments to commemorate, damage, and acknowledge the ordinary. With a lot of cold, dark, days, the straightforward act of lighting a candle and appreciating a mug of coffee might make a huge difference to one's spirit.

By having basic rituals without effort, the Danish people see both the residential and individual life as a form of art, and there is not a grind to avoid due to its significance. They incorporated hygge right into their everyday life, and hence it came to be a natural expansion rather than a forced or difficult event.

Hygge is as Danish as "aebleskiver" (a famous Danish recipe) and it goes far in lighting up the Danish heart. Hygge indicates creating a warm environment and enjoying the good things in life with good people.

Hygge includes basic practices such as

- The warm glow of candlelight.
- Cozying up with a loved one for a motion picture.

- Being around people you love is just nothing, but the best way you could practice hygge.
- Reviewing the small and huge points in life.

This clarifies why the Danish people are among the happiest individuals worldwide.

You can consider making it a daily practice with your friends and relatives, early in the morning and cozy evenings, and lighting candles on every dish.

Hygge can be explained simply as a hug, "That comfy a sensation that you obtain when you engage in the experiences that make you linked and truly pleased," discusses Adina Mahalli, certified psychological health, and wellness specialist and a family treatment professional with Maple Holistic.

There's nothing extravagant about hygge. It is more straightforward to the enjoyment and a much deeper feeling of satisfaction and excitement.

Regardless of whether it is the winter or summer season, there is always a good time for friends to take tea together, have long walked, practice bike riding, and do things just for the delight of it.

Citing Linda Lauren, an entrepreneur, and writer, "Living the Hygge lifestyle means that you will include a conscious indulgence while in comfy clothes and candle lights lit, an excellent book beside you and some calmness to take pleasure in."

"In Denmark, we have this principle of hygge," says Christian Hanson, a Danish cheesemaker based in Greenville, South Carolina who has Blue Ride Creamery. "Here in the States, it's generally converted as the adjective cozy." While comfort is certainly an essential part of its meaning, hygge is a verb. A writer by the name of Hanson states that "The act of developing the shared sensation of something in between satisfaction and happiness." Cocktails by a barking fire on a winter night set the mood for hygge. However, it also involves having a company have a shared experience.

"There is this sensation, something predominantly 'hyggelic' that comes from sharing great food with others," claimed Hanson. It's rooted in the basic spirit of supplying nutrition and hospitality.

Hanson also claims that "When you're a cheesemaker, it may take months and occasionally years, till you reach the taste your production. When you have finally reduced right into this wheel of cheese that you've formed, brined, flipped, cleaned, and doted on for so long, and when that cheese has developed to the best possible expression of the milk that it began from, and then you get to share that with others ... for me, that's the best expression of hygge," claims Hanson.

The history of the hygge lifestyle

It is an amusing concept that the Norwegians still use this word but with a more casual significance. What is even funnier is that the Norwegians after giving this precious gift to the Danish people, still needed to develop their word to describe hygge: koselig (close to the English "cozy" however most likely no linguistic link).

Although hygge stems from Norway (as a word), it was the Danish people who offered it an entire brand-new twist, making it the most distinct element of Danish society. And a worldwide fad, as well!

The word appeared in Danish works in the late 18th and very early 19th century and has since then been embraced as a Danish culture and art of life. Both words have a similar meaning in both countries. Both the Old Danish people and Norwegians engaged in the concept as early as the 18th century.

Similar to the German principle of 'gemütlichkeit' and the Dutch suggestion of 'gezelligheid', the comfortable and warm way of life that hygge promotes has been an essential part of Danish culture. It is stemmed from a Norwegian word for "well-being," as stated above).

While hygge-- which is applied both as a noun and an adjective in Denmark—it's not just a way of life for the Denmark people, it has eventually gained its popularity in the UK in 2016 after several books regarding the subject were published. It came to be so popular in Britain, to the point that it was listed in the Collins Words of the Year for 2016-- second only to Brexit.

Pinterest predicted that it would undoubtedly be one of the most popular home design fads of 2017 after the task on the site concerning "hygge" boosted 285 percent at the end of 2016. To date, people have marked more than 4 million messages on Instagram with #hygge and have likewise taken to Twitter to talk about the finer points of what makes something hygge or not.

Significance of Hygge

I am sure that by now you have understood the art of Hygge and had an overview taste of how. Let's look into details on the importance of practicing this lifestyle.

To begin with, Hygge makes you slow down and enjoy the moment. When you exercise hygge, you are in the minute (you are mindful), forgetting your concerns.

Rather than 'postponing' when to enjoy your life, you discover the joy in the little things in life when you exercise hygge, which makes you a pleased and happy content individual.

We indeed have our ups and downs in life but through the art of Hygge, one can embrace every little joyful moment and aspect. Therefore, the difficulties are not able to overrule your life and judgments. You become grateful for the little opportunities and things that are around you and enjoy the moments with your friends and relatives. Remember, Hygge can be exercised from anywhere.

When you think about it, life is made up of all these little moments? You have only this minute with you and hygge shows you to make a lot of it by being happy

Besides, Danish people practice hygge as a means to escape the lengthy winter. There are comparable practices around the globe understood under different names. You don't have to restrict hygge only in the winter season. As described, Hygge can be practiced at any time of the year, month, and day.

Hygge is enjoying the little moments of life by being connected. In other words, the season or area does not matter as long as you can locate a method to bring hygge to your life.

1

THE BASIC ESSENTIALS OF HYGGE

Hygge essentials

a) Living Lights

Most Danes say that they associate hygge with a good overwhelming percentage mentions candles. The faster way to get hygge is to light a few candles or, what they say in Danish, "living lights" or 'levende Lys',

b) Something Sinful

The level of meat and coffee consumption in many areas in Denmark is linked to hygge. Hygge is all about personal and giving yourself a better treatment, and giving each other, a break from the demands of healthy living. Some foods like Cake are 'hyggeligt' compared to those foods that are not sweet. Others include coffee or hot chocolate is 'hyggeligt'. Others like Carrot sticks are not so much hyggeligt. Something sinful is a part of the hygge ritual. But it should not be something fancy or extravagant. But a hearty stew is hyygeligt. Popcoons are hyggeligt especially when sharing the sme bowl.

c) Sharing chores

Hygge is a situation where there is a lot of relaxed thoughtfulness. Nobody should take center stage or dominates the conversation for a longer period. Equality is a good element in hygge, a trait that is deeply known in the Danish culture—and also manifests itself in the fact that everybody participates in the chores of the hyggeligt during the evening. It is more hyggeligt if we all help each other to prepare food, instead of one doing it alone in the kitchen.

d) Reminiscence planning

Hygge may help us to be better every day because it is about savoring simple pleasures. Hygge is also a way of planning for and preserving happiness for many Danes. Danes plan for hyggeligt times and reminisce about them afterward.

e) A Nook to Snuggle Up In

Every home needs a hyggekrog, which translates as "a nook." It is the place in the room where you love to relax with a blanket, a book, and a cup of tea.

Danes love their comfy spaces. Everyone wants one, and 'hyggekroge' is common in Copenhagen and most countries. By walking on the streets of the city, you will notice that many buildings have bays on the window. On the inside, these are almost certainly filled with cushions and blankets, providing the people who live there with a cozy place to sit and relax after a long day.

f) Togetherness

On average, most Europeans interact and socialize with friends, family, or colleagues on most days of the week. The corresponding average in Denmark is around 78 percent.

Spending time with other people creates an atmosphere that is warm, relaxed, friendly, down-to-earth, close, comfortable, and welcoming. In many cases, it is like a good hug but without physical contact. In this situation, you can completely relax. The art of hygge is therefore also the art of expanding your comfort zone to include other friends.

Things that you need for the art of Hygge

a. SOFT LIGHTS:

Candles are good components of a hygge lifestyle. You can easily use them to retain warmth and ambiance in your house. Try things like tea lights scattered across a mantel or console table, and use pillars or hurricanes as a flickering centerpiece. room. You may also try using an array of flickering candles in various sizes to create the perfect balance of lighting pillar, tea light, and hurricane.

Brilliant lights are not hyggeligt. Dimmer lights are recommended. Many Danish people connect candles with hygge. It is estimated that every Denmark citizen burns at least 6 kilos of candlelight wax annually. However, the Danish people may be overwhelmed by light due to the chilly, dark winter seasons and short summer periods. This is another reason why hygge is such a fundamental part of their culture.

b. FOOD:

Hygge often focuses on great food with great company. Something wicked is an indispensable element of the hygge ritual. Do not feel guilty concerning being kind to yourself when in a while with sweet treats or baked products. It can be anything, yet preparing them on your own or with the company of someone raises the hygge-factor than purchasing from the shop. Don't you love the scent of increasing bread in the stove that loads your cooking area? Hygge is all about appreciating such wonderful moments. When you bear in mind such moments, you realize you don't require many things before you can be contented in life.

Beverages like tea, coffee, delicious hot chocolate are also essential for the art of hygge. Specifically, in the cool months, the warmth provided by a warm drink is a reward.

c. VISIBILITY:

Hygge is all about valuing the easy pleasures of life by living in the minute. It is simply being conscious and being present. Switch off your phones and other disturbances. Try to delight your inner soul in the hygge activity you choose for a full experience of Hygge.

d. HYGGEKROG:

'Hyggekrog' can be translated as a cozy space. Make your cozy corners in your house by putting some cushions, coverings, or anything you can connect with coziness or leisure after a long day.

e. BOOKS:

Have a collection of publications that you wish to read and go through. Fiction books and novels can entertain you while a good self-help publication/book will always have a thing or two to teach you.

If you love books as I do, we can agree that taking time reading a publication is just one of the most effective hyggeligt experiences. Publications can take you to another world of imagination and realization while just seated on your couch enjoying a cup of hot cocoa. It lets your imagination cut loose and can take away your worries for a short time. As the saying by Mason Cooley goes, "reading provides someplace to go when we have to stay where we are."

f. BLANKETS AND CUSHIONS:

To have a cozy space in your home, place some cushions and toss coverings in your hygge area. Cushions and pillows generally make people comfortable. So you can use them while consuming alcohol or a hot favorite after a tiresome day. Or put them on your lap for relaxing your hands while reading a book. Toss covering maintains your coziness and sense of relaxation.

g. GOOD COMPANY:

While you can hygge on your own, hygge mainly takes place in small groups of close friends or household.

There is a straight connection between the quality of your partnerships and joy. The more you hang around with individuals near to you, the extra unwanted and happy you can feel. Great conversations with excellent food in an ambiance are helpful for your psychological wellness, which's why Hygge is ranked as a crucial factor in Danish individuals' trick of joy.

H. CLOTHES THAT ARE COZY:

Ordinary Changing into your pajamas, from

your normal day clothing by itself, is hyggeligt. Ah, that relief!

To make it through the chilly winter season, you require hand-knit woolen sweaters, scarves, and socks, and has several layers of garments as you want. Wear what is informal and comfortable. Select light-tinted loosened cotton clothing if it is summer. Basically, gown for the climate without reducing any form of coziness from the setting.

I. WATCHING MOVIES OR PLAYING BOARD GAMES:

If you want to experience hygge, opting out of the online globe is necessary. For this reason, you have to discover activities to involve on your own and if you have guests or your friends came around. It's high time that you play an old parlor game. It can be a positive experience to experience excellent old memories again. Or dim the lights and view your preferred film or Netflix reveal with your friends. You can light some candle lights to include extra hygge to your night

Non-essential elements of Hygge

It's not just done during winter.

You can practice hygge living in the summertime. Do things that make you feel great? Take an outing into the park or comfy up at a drive-in theater to enjoy a movie.

Relax a bonfire on the coastline and enjoy the audios of the collapsing waves while taking pleasure in the business of liked ones. Do anything straightforward that makes you feel great.

It denies things that compromise your focus to obtain that comfortable sensation.

Hygge is about creating a certain environment-- it is not concerning purchasing things. It has to do with creating gratitude for the small things in life that make you happy. It is a lot more about the simplistic nature of being. So you don't require to buy anything you don't already have to exercise this lifestyle.

It's not a reason for slouching or binge eating.

Yes, hygge focuses on fitting. Moreover, your

costume is an integral part of developing a comfortable atmosphere too. Self-made rewards, comfort food, and warm beverages are all very reassuring points. However, the idea of hygge is more about comfort and experience.

Possibly you appreciate your mom's old delicious chocolate chip cookie recipe to feel this sense of convenience. But that is just a tiny part of this way of life. Yes, take pleasure in that piece of cake that someone is passing over to you. But if you want to feel your ideal physically, you still should maintain healthy consumption in mind, so moderation is still key.

It's not a reason to brag to others about your success.

Hygge is about really feeling good, not feeling inferior, or making others feel that way. It has to do with investing quality time with individuals you like and making them feel as good as you feel. It motivates both modesty and synergy and shies away from extremes. Hygge embraces fairness, equality, and a requirement for consensus.

2

THE PROCEDURE UPON THE PRACTICE OF THE ART OF HYGGE

After the heat of the summer has faded, sometimes it is good to stay appealing than staying home and curling up in cozy warmth.

People create a cozy, friendly space perfectly suited for enjoying the simple pleasures of life with others and the family. This process is described by Germans as gemütlichkeit, and also in Scotland, the word is còsagach. This concept is taking off as people in colder climates embrace the mindset and welcome the winter months. Follow our guides filled with tips for creating the perfect hygge lifestyle and also to try a perfect hygge

Creating a feeling of hygge does not have to take a lot of effort, cash, or time. There is nothing fancy, costly, or lavish about a pair of hideous woolen hygge socks-- and that is an essential feature of hygge.

The ideal day of hygge is to make sure that you have adequate time, not be in a rush, and concentrate on the straightforward pleasures. For circumstances, allow an excellent stew to simmer for hours. While you read an excellent book and take pleasure in a nice mug of tea.

Below are some of the ways in which you can integrate hygge into your way of living:

1. Associate yourself with people.

Hygge is the method of making any type of provided moment comfortable and intimate. At often, when enjoyed ones get together for a social occasion, they do so to experience the link, warmth, and joy of the occasion. Hygge is largely a social undertaking, the finest appreciated in the company of other individuals.

Uplifting people is another great use of hygge. Bake something and come by a pal's home that you haven't seen in a while to hang around with each other and indulge in hygge living with each other. Togetherness is a huge part of hygge. Host a movie evening or get together with your closest good friends for an intimate supper.

Or, if you want to obtain very hygge, you cannot do much better than developing fire in the wintertime and cozying up to it with your enjoyed ones. If you include hot drinks and warm coverings, Fireside is the utmost hygge shelter-- specifically.

2. Give yourself some time to relax.

People are hurrying from one area time-to-time to the following. There is always someplace that we need to be, and we are regularly thinking about the points on our to-do lists. To hygge accurately, you require to let on your own kick back and give on your own time to take it all in. Taking your time when it comes to relaxing and enjoy your early morning coffee. Take your time to relish the dinner that you worked so hard to make. If you want some relaxing tasks that you can do, start with knitting. This craft has a soothing high quality in it, and you can be productive and relax at the same time while you knit things for your loved ones.

Learning to loosen up can be life-altering': just how to discover your comfort area

Just how do you like to kick back, relax, and actually kick back? This appears as if it needs to be a basic question. I can't be alone in having actually spent several nights over the past couple of weeks slumped on the sofa, "seeing TV" while my eyes flicker throughout Twitter and Facebook, and five various WhatsApp teams on my phone.

Kicking back is increasingly challenging in our always-on electronic world. When I discover myself at the house with a totally reluctant evening, at times I don't get an idea what to do. However, finish up looking emptily at one screen or additional hours, before stumbling off to bed, wondering where the time has gone.

This appears to be typical trouble. Elon Musk, when asked what he normally does after the job, said: "Usually function even more"-- which does not appear to be thriving for him.

The demand for some simple resource of relaxation can be seen in the initial rise in popularity of the adult coloring publication. In addition to last year's 13.3% rise in sales of books providing spiritual advice on exactly how to reside in a busy globe, and the mindfulness "mega pattern" seen in Headspace, the meditation application that has been downloaded and installs more than 15m times. Those people who spent our cash on these items were probably searching for a solution to a few of the very same inquiries-- and most of us are still looking. The bottom has currently left of the coloring book market, with Forbes stating it "dead" in May, and, in June in 2015, Headspace laid off 13 team members.

According to a report by Ofcom one summertime: "Most people in the UK depend on their digital gadgets and desire a continuous connection to the internet." It discovered that 78% of people currently possess a smartphone-- rising to 95% of 16- to 24-year-olds. We inspect these phones generally every 12 minutes of our waking lives, with 54% of us really feeling that the gadgets interrupt our conversations with loved ones, and 43% of people really feeling that we invest way too much time online. We can't kick back with them, and we do not recognize just how to unwind without them. 7 in 10 people never ever turn them off.

The medical psychologist Rachel Andrew says she sees the issue daily in her consulting room, and it is worsening. "I've discovered a rise in my practice, certainly over the last three to 5 years, of people discovering it increasingly hard to switch off and unwind. And it's across the lifespan, from age 12 to 70," she claims. The same issues come up again and again: modern technology, phones, work e-mails, and social networks.

Kicking back in front of one display or one more does have its place, says Andrew-- but it depends how you do it.

"Sometimes individuals describe not being engaged in what they're checking out-- completely out, not knowing what they've been doing for the last half-hour, that's what happens when your mind is very exhausted it takes itself out of the situation. That's not likely to be beneficial by any means."

That is why, after I have actually spent a night looking emptily at Twitter, or leaving before the TV-- less Netflix and chill, more Netflix and nap-- I wake up feeling as if I have actually consumed a lot of convenience food. I have puzzled feeling brain-dead with really feeling kicked back.

The Institute of Psychoanalysis psychoanalyst David Morgan thinks that for many of us, this deadening resort to our screens is both a reason for and a repercussion of the truth that we no more understand how to relax and appreciate ourselves. Our displays and what we utilize them for are all techniques of disturbance, he claims. "People have got so utilized to seeking disturbance that they, in fact, cannot stand a night with themselves. It is a method of not seeing oneself, due to the fact that to have insight right into oneself needs mental space, and all these distraction methods are used as a method of avoiding obtaining close to the self."

Several of her patients, Andrew discusses, simply never navigate to thinking of how they wish to spend their time. "People state they are so hectic doing the 'should,'" she states. Whether that is functioning, caring for the household, or being a part of requiring friendships-- that by the time an evening or weekend break happens when they could do what they want, there is no power or inspiration left for anything yet "tumbling out." For other people the idea of getting in line with their very own needs and desires is alien, says Andrew. "It might genuinely be something they've never ever taken into consideration in the past," she claims.

One more issue is that it can be complicated to disentangle our very own desires from those of the people around us, states Nina Grunfeld, the founder of Life Clubs, an organization that aims to help individuals live more rewarding lives. "When my partner and I were fresh," she states, "we went to Rome on a break, and he wanted to be able to go to every chapel, every dining establishment, plus-everything."

It was just after coming to recognize myself, after assuming about my life without him and what I like as a specific. I recognized that, for me to appreciate a holiday and to come back feeling loosened up and refreshed, I need to read and be still.

I think back to just how I used to pass my time when I was young. The silent times sitting checking out a publication, the rowdier times baking with close friends. I resolve to make even more time to do the grown-up variations of these things over the next year-- from only after realizing that I started making justifications.

The reality is, I do all those perfect things sometimes now. But in some cases, it feels as if being in the globe is excessive, and I need to disappear from it by shedding myself on a screen. It is as if I long for that brain-dead feeling, even though I recognize it isn't good for me. Having psychoanalytic psychotherapy is aiding me to think of the reasons that I could do this. For Morgan, therapy can be a critical path out of being stuck in a screen-gazing rut. Because it is someplace an individual is motivated to use his/her mind.

"The healing room is the reverse of diversion-- it's concentration," he states. "When people enter my consuting space, they frequently inform me it's the very first time they have ever before felt they have had a room where they can't flee from points."

"We have all these several methods of distracting yourself from the most critical reality of life-- that people are living, and then we expire. Having a mind to help you consider points; having a person that can think deeply about things with you is a way to deal with this very frightening truth of life."

The other hand of that frightening fact is, naturally, the realization that because we don't have much time on this planet, it is an embarrassment to throw away any one of it voluntarily making ourselves brain-dead.

Leisure pointers

If you are hanging out with friends or family over the cheery duration, Nina Grunfeld advises designating everyone one hour in which they are in charge of the group's timetable. When they can choose whichever activity they think about is the most soothing. "One of my kids may determine we all need to play a video game; another will choose we are all choosing a walk; another will make us all cook cakes. That way you all get a little bit of 'me-time', and you can experience another person's and it's very kicking back not needing to make decisions for the entire day," she states.

It could be that you can't bear in mind, in addition to request friends or family, or even check out old photo CDs. In case you loved playing within the sandpit, you may possibly want to try art. And if you enjoyed building things, you might well want to make a loaf of bread.

Experiment with looking at the globe in a new way. "Allow on your own to discover. Walk anywhere you see and are what you can find that is entirely brand-new. Try to get lost-- whenever you reach a turning, ask yourself, do you wish to go left or right, and see where you wind up," says Grunfeld.

If you have no concept of just how to begin loosening up, check out the science. Many people recommend being out in nature is uplifting and beneficial."

Try doing some yoga if knitting really isn't your thing. It will help you to unwind your muscle mass literally. In an addition, it will give you a long time to launch your thoughts and tension, which is all a part of sensation comfortable in life.

Have a schedule: The very first action to give yourself a lot more leisure time is to figure out where you can make space in your timetable. "Evaluate your schedule to figure out what's squandering your time or energy," says health coach Jill Ginsberg over email.

Outsource some help for various activities: Sometimes, we can't do every little thing ourselves, and there are times when we require to put another person on a task to give ourselves that spare time. "Redistributing several of your work will free up your time and permit you to concentrate some of that extra time on preserving your health and wellness and relaxing," claims Ginsberg. "Delegate right stuff you despise doing or are awful at doing and focus on what you do best."

Limit yourself and do not overwork: "Don't take on even more than you can take care of," asserted Ginsberg; claiming 'yes to every little thing only produces even more anxiety'.

Focus on Your Breath: If you do not have time for a full-on health facility day, you can take a few mins any type of where you are simply to focus on your breath. "This workout can be done at your work desk or even in a stressful conference," says meditation educator and massage therapy specialist Kathleen Lisson over email. "Take a slow-moving deep inhale with your nose, then breathe out with your nose. Matter to 2, after that inhale again. Stopping briefly in between breaths brings leisure."

Take An Electronic Time Out: You're not genuinely kicking back if you're browsing through social networks or checking emails. Set aside time where you aren't participating in display time of any type of kind. "If that means retreating to the restroom to get some peaceful, or walking the border of your work environment, or simply providing yourself a 'break,' you will see advantages," says Sulack over email.

Laughing: either you take a couple of mins

enjoying an amusing YouTube video, chatting with friends, or thinking about a funny memory, allow yourself a good laugh. Giggling can help in reducing tension, soothe stress, stimulate your organs, alleviate discomfort. It also improves your body's immune system, according to Mayo Clinic.

Creating a space

Hygge is used to emphasize enjoyment in the simple pleasure of life. You can find a place in your home that is perfect for cuddling up. This may be near the fireplace, in a reading nook with a lot of natural lights, or simply in your bed. Next, gather the essentials for a cozy space. Hygge is all about enjoying the comforts of your own home and you'll need a few pieces to get started. Set the stage for a cozy night in with chunky knit blankets, soft acrylic throws, and plush velvet pillows. Soft sheepskin rugs and pillows add an undeniable sense of luxury that's approachable yet indulgent.

Embrace some Nap Time: "Setting aside 20 to half an hour for an adult snooze offers substantial health and wellness advantages, including improved performance, alertness, and power, while preventing a groggy duration after the remainder," states Dr.

Tieraona Low Dog, a chief clinical police officer of Well & Being over email. "Find a silent place to clear up in, get comfy and utilize an eye mask to keep brilliant lights at bay during your snooze. Remember to set an alarm system on your phone for

20 to 30 minutes so you do not sleep in. You will certainly awaken freshened, renewed, and all set to tackle the world."

Embrace taking a Shower: Everyone has to shower, so rather than making it a task, make it a sacred time on your own. Use your time to be conscious of just how your mind and body really feel, and even take into consideration making use of some aromatherapy for even more relaxation.

Develop Systems That Free Up Your Time: Don't squander your time repeating the exact same tasks. "Put your life on the auto-pilot by automating things like bill paying, transferring your checks utilizing your phone, create reoccurring orders for your household things, and setting up your computer to do weekly backups," claims Life Train - Amanda Sowadski over email.

Make An Appointment With Yourself: Learn to set up in "you-time" as if it was equally important like a conference with your employer. "If you create personal time on your timetable similarly you do visits with others, you'll be more probable actually to do it," claims Tina B. Tessina, Ph.D. over e-mail. "Join a class or team that fulfills consistently for a relaxing task such as Tai, dancing or yoga chi, or timetable a regular massage, manicure or face, so you'll have a guaranteed area to kick back."

3. Create some time to connect with nature.

Hygge living is typically linked with interior

tasks. It also involves utilizing your detects to have an appreciation for the noises, experiences, scents, and views of nature. Grab your friends and go out to your regional park to have an outing or play a video game of flag football.

Or, take some time to loosen up and lay out in the cozy sunlight with your preferred book and an ice-cold drink to practice hygge living when it is warm exterior. You can likewise take your dishes outside right into your lawn to get the most benefits from the sunlight before the winter months comes. It's time to conclude back inside.

During the winter months, you might not have the ability to find a great deal of greenery outside. You can still bring nature inside your home to brighten up your living room. Open the home window tones and maintain some potted plants inside your house to live a much more hygge way of living.

You can additionally include wood accents to your residence to make it a lot more in tune with nature. Think wood floors, tables, chairs-- all of these accents in your residence will make you feel a bit better to nature, which is an important part of hygge.

How to connect with nature.

What are we doing? We are spending endless hrs. in cool rooms, with neon lighting, before the displays, in huge states. The depression slips in. We begin really feeling unpleasant, relatively with no special cause. We break (or ought to I say, neglect) our bond with nature and we begin feeling shed.

The excellent information is that we can constantly notice this and go back to the roots. We can revive the link with nature (and, so the connection with our own nature). We can accept this wonderful connection and end up being better and much more based.

You might believe that reconnection with nature implies that you have to move to Kilimanjaro for six months. Heck no. Reconnection with nature can be quick, easy, and available to everyone each day. Here are ten suitable and fast concepts on how to connect with nature and be better.

1. Take a breath with the trees

Whenever you breathe out, the plants and trees are breathing. And when you do the same, plants and trees are taking their breath out too. This breathing workout will certainly assist you not just loosen up; however, connecting with nature in no time.

2. Walk barefoot

The ground likewise soaks up complimentary electrons via our feet, which has an antioxidant result. All of this should be sufficient inspiration for you to take off your shoes and take huge actions towards the yard, sandy coastline, or nearby park and reconnect with Mother Earth.

3. Grow a garden/plant

My story of the mushroom farm provides a powerful example of how mindful observation of a life cycle fosters happiness and the connection with nature. I have a veggie subscription at the neighboring ranch. It is excellent because it gives many great benefits without essential tough work. So you can take this choice into your consideration too! You can constantly go to a park and see what is going on with the plants on a routine basis.

4. Play with a pet dog

Pet dogs are amazing and lively and adorable and funny and they have their very own personalities and come across each minute with pleasure. They likewise remind us to do the same. Each animal personifies various merits and qualities that originate from Mother Nature. Pets advise us exactly how to be much better humans. Foster caring partnerships with family pets and various other pets and you will be better and extra meeting.

5. Eat seasonally

We've jointly been combating to have all types of food offered on the shelves of Walmart year long. And we made it. We can get virtually anything at any moment of the year. Other than that it sucks. Watermelons that you buy around Christmas (presuming that you survive in the Northern hemisphere) have actually taken a trip fifty percent of the globe to get where you are.

They have lots of chemicals and chemicals that maintain them in a good condition. Not to even mention the gas consumption needed for their transportation. It's not a very eco-friendly eating alternative.

Go to your farmers' market and get the stuff that is currently in season. Now is the ideal time for watermelons, bananas, corn, asparagus, peaches, and several even more goodies. When we are eating seasonally, we are lessening our effects on the environment. We are eating much healthier and we are linking with nature.

6. Honor the periods

In our lives, we additionally have periods and phases. Our lives are rather series of stages and cycles and seasons, odd, warped spirals in which we duplicate the lessons and become that we are. Why do we then expect to really feel the same method and do the same things no matter the season? Let's reconnect with nature and acknowledge in which period we are in. Let's accept the charm and the transience of each period. And after that, we can let it go and shift to a new period gracefully and embrace its beauty.

7. Reduce.

Everything in nature takes place slowly, slowly, and without a battle. Nature is never in a rush and always obtains everything done. You can't connect with nature if you are still running at that speed of life. Just try to discover how to reduce down and dive into the present moment.

Water your garden carefully and without a thrill, like it's not simply another duty on your to-do checklist. To attach to nature we have to tune right into its gentle and positive pace.

8. Sit by the water.

9. Take photos.

Digital photography is an amazing practice that makes us value the aesthetic appeal of the world around us. In the beginning, an image named "Nature" and record whatever in nature grabs your focus. Fallen leaves, blossoms, trees, birds, butterflies, pets, beaches, landscapes, and sundowns, nothing can escape your attraction.

10. Pertain to your senses and take pleasure in.

Mother Nature pleases all of our five senses; all we have to do is to listen. We already discussed visual beauty in suggestion # 9. Take your earphones out and pay attention to birds, crickets, and the wind in the covers of the plants. Experience the aroma of lavender, pine trees, and the ocean under the radiations of the sunlight. Touch the tree bark, try to feel the breeze in your hair and the yard underneath your bare feet (concept 2). Take a good bite of juicy watermelon (suggestion 5). Reconnection along with nature is actually the formation of multi-dimensional encounters. Involve your five senses and take pleasure in every degree.

11. Take value in the simple factors of life

Hygge residing is actually all about ease. It has to do with finding delight in little, daily moments as opposed to looking for delights or outrageous experiences to feel happy. You do not need to remodel your entire home to make it a lot more compatible with a hygge way of living.

By making some little enhancements, you can transform your minutes in the house from being lackluster to be intimate and joyful. For example, treating on your own to your favored coffee, finding a new sort of bath salt or bubble bath so that you can kick back in the bathtub. Otherwise, placing your preferred photos in structures around your residence can also be a unique form of hygge. Considering that they can elevate your mood rapidly, all of these small points are equally considerable and credible to you feel good.

The one-of-a-kind feature of hygge is that no matter how hard you might attempt, you cannot buy your way into it. This is really the factor. When you have actually effectively attained hygge, it indicates that you have decreased and simplified your life.

Hygge is not about material things. Instead, it is a detailed mindset that focuses on comfort. It depends on you to create those moments by allowing on your own to stop and appreciate the things around you.

When you're drinking your early morning coffee

or such a moment that you first creep into bed at night-- take a minute to feel the comfort in depth. In addition, try to make use of each of your senses to create an experience for yourself that is memorable and makes you delighted.

Simply, stop recognizing the delight of the easy things in your life. The border on your own with only things that really bring you pleasure. Hygge is nothing about overindulgence. So, take pleasure in the simplicity of your environments and utilize your home for living as opposed to a place to save your points.

We do not identify them properly, neglect them, or simply take them for granted. We forget them, and that's an important error.

In reality, these little things have a substantial influence on our lives. That's why we must discover to identify their worth.

A guide to taking value and appreciating the simple values in life

1. Be Creative

Hygge is all about taking it easy and enjoying the current state of life around your atmosphere. It is a good time to learn a craft, such as knitting or crocheting. If crafting is not your style, consider baking. Freshly-made sweet treats or homemade bread fill the air with pleasing aromas.

1. Little Indulgences

Whether it's a glass of hot tea with cardamom or a mug of mulled wine, a warm drink brings you perfectly in line with the hygge lifestyle. Hygge is all about doing the things that make you happy, so yes — allow yourself to indulge in all types of threats. Fresh pastries or other comforting foods are perfect for keeping the mood. Allow yourself small luxuries for home decor as well. Adorn side tables in family rooms with special photos of friends and family in stylish frames. In some cases, you can add a delicate potted plant in a gorgeous pot to a sunny window sill. You can also Fill decorative bowls on coffee, console tables with fragrant and colorful potpourri to enchant multiple senses.

Valuing the little points in life indicates that you focus your attention on what nurtures and sustains you in life. On everything that brings you also the smallest quantity of pleasure.

It also suggests practicing thankfulness by discovering these everyday things that you consider provided so easily.

By valuing small things in life, you won't quit poor things from happening. However, you'll need to discover how to stop emphasizing the definition of poor occasions to your life.

You'll locate an important resource of psychological balance.

2. Why establish the skill of gratefulness?

Abilities in experiencing and revealing gratefulness are essential for getting in touch with other people.

Once you take a moment to value the acts of compassion coming from somebody either known or unknown to you, you'll become a lot more aware of your coming from a neighborhood of people who care about each other.

Reciprocating these actions assists to enhance these social bonds. They produce a source on which you can draw in times of demand.

This sort of good feeling has been actually linked to physical health and wellness.

A positive way of thinking aids the immune system of your body and quickens recuperation time. Favorable emotions additionally aid us to be extra innovative and resourceful.

Durable individuals construct their strengths on positive feelings. These feelings merely help them to deal with tight spots.

By learning how to appreciate the little points in life, you'll have the ability to enhance the existence of favorable feelings in your life and reap the benefit.

Right here's exactly how to include gratitude right into your regimen

a) Maintain a 'Gratefulness journal'

It's worth keeping an appreciation journal.

Academic studies on the field reveal that individuals who have such journals for tape-recording daily true blessings have a much more optimistic sight of their lives. They tend to experience an extra positive state of mind and exercise a lot more.

Spend 10 or 15 minutes daily on listing things for which you feel thankful. It's just how you can enhance your appreciation for the little things that you generally overlook.

b) Create a bulletin board

This is where you can put up little reminders of points that make you feel thankful. It can be everything from a thank-you note from a customer to a transcribed character from a close friend.

At the end of the year, take each of these down and submit all of them in a particular thankfulness directory. By doing so, you can have a look at your year at any time to see how blessed you are.

c) Celebrate the little things

Offer yourself consent to do that. Here's how you can celebrate your small victories in life:

Celebrate a good climate by getting a good friend and going with a walk;

When somebody around you masters a brand-new skill, provide a little existing to commemorate their success; Commemorate getting through a complicated job by doing something you enjoy.

d) Send out one email of gratitude a time

Make it a practice to send out one thank-you e-mail to an individual every day. Try not to add more than one significant and engaging sentence in it, otherwise, it would lose its credibility.

You'll feel the energy of his process when your partnerships and social life start to end up being more satisfying.

e) Slow down your life

You must appreciate it as a lot as you can when you're in the middle of an amazing event.

Right here are some wise means to help you obtain one of the most out of these pleasant emotions:

Keep a significant souvenir of the experience to aid yourself recall the memory in the future;

Become part of the favorable experience with all your detects; Keep an eye on details; Share this experience with others-- as it takes place, or by thinking back later on.

f) Keep your existence remarkable

Select to be existing in the current situations. This sort of awareness of the minute-- occasionally called mindfulness-- is vital to generating favorable feelings that come with appreciation.

When you're coping with more understanding, you notice every little thing-- even the little pieces of day-to-day elegance.

You can value the here and now moment by utilizing previous individual difficulties. Rather than dwelling on adverse emotions, recall them and you're bound to feel how points are much better now.

g) Be conscious of your most valued things

Think of that somebody asks you concerning one of the most important points in life. You need to have a clear response to this question. It's an indicator that you're out of touch with on your own if you do not.

Link to what's vital to you, and don't put it off till life gets less busy. Trust me, it never does.

h) Fall asleep with gratefulness

Ideally, you need to awaken and go to bed with gratitude at the core of your mind and deep inside your heart.

Start completing your day with favorable emotional aids to construct a balanced life. Gradually, it will pave the way towards healthy sleep at the end of the day.

It's probably because your mind is still weighing over the demanding events of the day if you're having difficulty dropping asleep at night.

As opposed to thinking of the things you need to do tomorrow, try to enter the gratitude mode at bedtime. Consider the attractive things that happened to you on that day.

Did you observe exactly how the snow broke under your feet? Or maybe you've identified a stunning ray of the sun filtered through the fallen leaves of a tree?

Try to welcome that retrospection as you drift off

to rest. You'll awaken sensation revitalized and energetic to take on the obstacles of the day.

5. Consciously choosing homemade over store-bought goods.

It ought to come as no surprise that Danish food has struck the worldwide cooking scene, particularly with the recent "farm-to-table" fad. When you prefer to make your own food as opposed to buying it, you can recognize precisely what you are taking into your body. And you can appreciate the fruits of your labor if you are the one cooking.

Naturally, comfort food is constantly a treat. However, there's something that is additionally satisfying for creating your home cooking from square one. And the fact is, creating staples like homemade poultry noodle soup is extremely simple. The fragrance of your childhood will certainly come rushing back into your house as soon as you get your energetic ingredients mixed up.

If you intend to create factors added hygge, visit a dish for 'ebelskivers'. This cross in between a popover along with a pancake is a timeless Danish bread that is actually often appreciated during opportunities of real hygge. Or even, if you remain in the mood to chill out along with an alcoholic drink, work up some blackberry glögg. In fact, it is an essential drink to someone who is looking for warmth and ease.

Add Softness

Developing a cozier area to relax can have a significant impact on your mood, your family members' mood, and the total sensation of your residence. It does not mean that you need to acquire a brand-new sofa either!

Pillows-- Pillows aren't just for the bedroom or couch! Create a comfortable corner with some natural floor pillows, bean bags, or yoga exercise reinforces. They motivate activity and play for the children and likewise make the ideal seat for playing family members' parlor game around the coffee table.

Throw coverings-- Layer them over the sofa or place them in a basket in each room. My children enjoy the softness of this blanket.

Select deep-pile carpets-- Choose a warm comfy throw rug to mash your toes into! Also, throw one over the back of a chair or on the sofa.

Enjoy the outdoors

Being outside is good for our mental and physical health and wellness-- a sensation that does not vanish throughout the cooler months. In fact, spending quality time outdoors during the winter might be especially essential in safeguarding us from seasonal depression.

To take hygge outside, get hold of some pals, and try out some adventurous winter months activities. Bundling up and heading out for a walk in nature, saturating up the crisp winter months air and smothered calm of a snow-covered landscape, can be incredibly invigorating.

6. Cozify Your Quarters the Hygge lifestyle

Just how do people loosen up throughout a polar vortex? Hyggeify your life. Get some satisfaction by organizing your areas. If you ask Marie Kondo, a decluttered house is a relaxing residence.

Maintain every little thing in place with baskets or containers that hold hygge basics like plush coverings. Think about storage ottomans or benches for added space. Decluttering is a simple way to locate daily ease and satisfaction.

You can additionally integrate contemporary furnishings with declaration pieces for a special yet minimal style. New furnishings is a worthwhile investment, yet you can maintain points affordable by purchasing from online furniture sellers with a lot of cozy and soft options.

Buffalo gingham, tartan, and check are popular patterns during chillier months for that cabin ambiance. Discover comfortable toss cushions or rugs in your preferred colors to take a snug sense to your home. Fill your area with parlor games and snacks, to make sure that whoever has the satisfaction of being your guest will certainly feel comfortable.

The Un-Hygge Way: Avoid treating your area as a discarding ground for arbitrary points: remove that only chair holding loads of washing or that pile of junk mail on your cooking area table. Your home ought to be more than a crash pad. Make it feel like a house, and you'll enter it blissfully at the end of daily.

Adding Hygge to your cleaning routine.

1) Smell.

Usage items that are natural and have fantastic aromas making use of essential oils. There's a distinction between cleaning your home windows utilizing a toxic spray cleaner that you inhale all those fumes or a natural spray with the aroma of Lemon Verbena floating via your areas.

Having a delicious-smelling house will certainly give you pleasing memories associated with cleansing.

2) Listen.

While you're cleansing save up those podcasts you've intended to pay attention to and submerge yourself in the various globe. Not only will you have a clean home, yet you'll be actually discovering something too.

3) Before & After.

Take a photo of the space before you begin cleaning up, and then take a photo of the room after you finish. Feel excellent about your success and maintain it as a suggestion of exactly how you would such as the room to stay.

4) Incentive.

Give yourself little incentives along the way.

After you finish cleaning up the refrigerator, consume that truffle you've been saving.

Decide ahead of time just how to split up the areas in your house and have your benefits currently picked for completing each job. Leave your favored benefit for last, when you end up the entire task.

5) Pair it up.

Invite one of your close friends over to help you and after that do the very same at her residence. Time will certainly go much faster as you catch up on each other's lives.

6) Blessings.

More than happy you have washing to well-maintained as it indicates that you possess family members to care for. Well-maintained those windows along with the expertise that you have a roofing system over your head that maintains you warm and comfortable and cozy.

7) Music notes.

Your home is your phase. Now is the moment where you check out those dance moves and sing on top of your lungs. Clean a time where you get to contact your inner rock celebrity and unleash.

8) Memory lane.

While you're cleansing and touching all the products in your house, why not decrease memory lane and keep in mind the special moments in your life where that item entered it.

As you do away with your plate, does it bring up

the minds of your granny offering you Sunday dinner on it? After dusting your crystal flower holder, your residence is full of treasured memories. Utilize your time cleaning those items as a way to heal your heart with your past.

9) Give.

Utilize your time cleaning up as a possibility to offer to others. As you clear out your closets, look for points you can contribute to those who are less fortunate in contrast to you.

10) Invite.

Strategy a fun gathering at your house total with board games and a pot luck food selection. There's nothing like the risk of a firm that will motivate you to make your home in great problem. The incentive is to enjoy your family and friends and making happy memories.

11) Timed event.

A timer will let you do tiny sections of cleaning each time. Cleaning a whole house does not sound like much fun. Cleaning for 10 minutes? That's practical. Go and set a timer!

12) Less = more.

It's much easier to clean up if you have much less to cleanse. Perfect reasoning, right? Strive to have better products in your home that you tend to make constant use of. Like a handmade offering bowl that a musician puts his or her heart right into it, etc.

If you spend your money on a higher value thing,

make sure you get one of the most of it by hosting tiny celebrations at your home.

7. The Aesthetics of Hygge Life

It's the little points that produce a space. Keep types straightforward and tidy while fostering a spirited spirit. Highlight your hobbies via decor and grow shared enjoyment. For instance, dart boards are an outstanding video game to participate in with guests. This wall deco works as a house good that shows your individuality.

If you gather something distinct, like vintage indications, put your collection on-screen as wall surface art. Maybe you play a tool as a leisure activity. Showcase the tool itself, or enhance with sheet music and verses that talk with your character.

Simplified accents such as pendant, floor, string, or table lights offer to set to an or else uncomplicated room. Candles are another fantastic way to tie in the atmosphere. Various other hygge life enhancements are natural herb and flavor yards and every sort of houseplant. Bring tranquility with life. If you like food preparation, try to showcase that you're fond of the freshness of your basil.

If you're not yet ready for a life partner, or a canine, or a high-maintenance plant, consider simple to take care of choices like jade, cacti, and succulents.

Think outside the package when presenting

greenery and usage rustic dangling pots or freestanding grid gardens.

The Un-Hygge Way: Find the balance between untidy messes and bland interiors. Hygge values minimalism and practicality while additionally valuing comfy personal contacts. Don't fill your area along with too much or spruce up along with so little bit of that it leaves you uninspired.

8. Attach

When it's blustery outside, we may be less likely to make social strategies. Nonetheless, Russell worries that wintertime supplies the best opportunity to "pull together at home and get hygge."

To transport Danish-style hosting, attempt not to bother your house being completely spotless or your food selection extravagantly attractive (a simple pot of soup is the best cold-weather remedy). This information, which is useless in the grand scheme of points, disrupts the real definition of hygge and hinders spontaneous events. To take the burnout of hosting also further, make your brunch or supper potluck-style, inviting your visitors to bring a favorite dish to share.

9. Learn to linger

Hygge is not something you can attain in a rush. It could be difficult for active Canadians to embrace it, but meddling in the art of sticking around enables us to slow down. Try to live even more mindfully, and uncover lots of hyggelig moments we could otherwise pass by.

If your regular possibility is to spring up after the foods to start cleaning up, make an effort rather rest for an instant and cherish the nutrients you gave your body. Staying around the desk with others, enjoying a mug of tea or glass of red wine, permits space for much deeper conversations to unravel.

10. The dressing art of Hygge

Staying relaxed does not just relate to your home. Bring hygge life and the sensation of a cozy hug into every aspect, including garments.

When venturing outdoors, remain elegant without giving up heat. There are extra alternatives than appearing like Yeti or fatality by cold. Winter season matches are particularly helpful in winter. Look for hefty fabrics like wool, tweed, and flannel. Maintain wardrobe shades wintery and timely with refreshing tones like oxblood, seeker eco-friendly, or cognac.

Layering clothing and investing in coats will aid you to stay relaxing during freezing months. When layering, keep in mind to focus on the base and mid-layers and the covering, after that complement with some shade and appearance. Pea overcoats, parkas, or coats are excellent additions to any kind of appearance.

11. Art of self-care through Hygge

Enjoying each and every bit of life is a Danish

staple indicating it's vital to maintain on your own in top-notch problems. There are a lot of manly possibilities to treat yourself.

Think about including a moisturizer to your cutting routine to maintain your skin smooth and secured from blustery weather conditions. Hit the health club for an invigorating workout to defeat the downturns and winter blues.

Loosen up by using your cost-free time to loosen up with a new film or get a new book and learn about an exciting brand-new subject. The alternatives are countless, so make self-care a top priority.

The Un-Hygge Way: Doing way too much might worry you out while doing too little falls leaves you feeling indifferent. Find composure and guarantee by maintaining a schedule and setup time aside for self-care tasks. And if possible, try striking the Juul a little much less.

Hygge and Ultimate Self-Care

There are reasons why Hygge has become the latest trend until today. We live in a busy world where carving out self-care for ourselves has been set aside. Hygge Ideas on Ultimate Self-Care will give you tips on making sure you take care of the most important person in your life - YOU!

It believes precisely what you inform it-- with the words you utilize to explain on your own, the activities you take to care for yourself, and the selections you make to share yourself. Inform the world that you are distinctive creation who came below to experience marvel and spread delight.

-- Victoria Moran, Lit From Within: Tending Your Soul for Lifelong Beauty

Given that you're looking to enhance your life with hygge ideas, I'm presuming you like all points of cozy living. How would your life change right if you had the ability to offer yourself the nutrition you need in every facet of your life?

A lot of us make sure everybody around us is caring for, but end up ignoring ourselves in the process.

Pointers of Ultimate Self-Care through Hygge:

1) Become your own friend.

Quit looking for that individual that will always sustain you. You currently located her or him, simply look in the mirror.

Learn to be your greatest follower. If you slip up, offer yourself words of encouragement. If others do not treat you properly, don't enable it. Recognize that you're an impressive person and supply the world with your presents.

2) Lead your life from the heart.

Your head will give you terrific advice, but your heart will constantly direct you in the ideal direction if you place your finest well-being.

Ensure that, all your future choices have created the life you always wanted to own and are not just the result of old habits.

3) Make your own food.

You know precisely what ingredients go into every bite when you make your very own recipes. Remember that restaurants and junk food locations do not always have your best interest in mind and sometimes utilize poor-quality components or include way too much salt to make their food taste much better.

Taking control of the fuel you utilize to power your body throughout the day will entirely change your life.

4) Beneficial drinks.

Rather than squandering vacant calories on beverages that damage, instead of recovering your body, change your drinks to ones that nourish your cells.

Consume natural herbal teas that assist your organs to do their job. You can make your very personal lemon ginger root tea-- food right here. However, you can also create your personal homemade warm cacao along with stevia, nuts dairy, and organic cacao.

I start on a daily basis currently with eco-friendly lemonade. I extract 2 apples, 2 lemons, one number of eco-friendlies, one cucumber, and half a number of oatmeal, and 1/4 of a fennel origin. It often creates one quart of extract and I drink all morning.

5) Continued education and learning.

Just because you finished senior high school or college, that does not imply you need to quit discovering.

Use your commute to function to listen to podcasts rather than music. Take that online training course that intrigues you. Sign up for proceeding education classes.

Purchase on your own, both for work and for pleasure.

6) Vision board.

Produce that vision board you've implied to do. Your dreams must be kept in front of you at all times. Refer to your board to be sure you're creating the best alternatives when you pertain to different forks on the highway. When you learn to self-nurture yourself, maintaining your desires at the best of your mind will definitely aid you to make the lifestyle you really want.

7) Less, but better.

Make sure you enjoy every post of clothes you have and that you're comfortable using them. If not, offer various other things you do not enjoy that much and make certain you're relaxing both in your home and in your closet.

8) Little deluxe.

Spoil on your own with high-grade cost-effective treats.

Buy impressive candlelight with a fragrance you love. How about this syrup-smelling candlelight with a wooden wick that sounds like a fireplace crackling. You can find one below.

Indulge in a small box of truffles when you get a sweet tooth.

9) Wrap yourself in nature.

Separating yourself from nature is harmful. Generate plants to your home and take place treks via the timbers every chance you obtain.

10) Release.

It's time to allow go of the people in your life that no longer offer your higher function. Equally, as you can have harmful items in your home, hazardous partnerships can be much more harmful.

11) Plan.

Have a strategy of how you intend to begin your day, just how you live your day, and just how you finish your day and attempt to persevere. See to it you load your day with generosity for yourself and others.

12) Magical moments.

Search for the amazing things that are going on in the world, and ignore the adverse. Seek those magic minutes in a smile, the clouds, or perhaps the gorgeous notes of a song.

5. The art of love through Hygge: Join In on cold Season

If you have not listened to it, it's cuffing period. "À la Lil' Wayne or you can welcome that love impends and obtain cozy with a unique someone.

Companionship is a major possession to including hygge. Turn that abstract cozy hug into a concrete one.

If you're coupled up already, cold weather can make it difficult to leave your residence or home. Think of ideas to maintain yourselves inhabited, like trying a new recipe or beginning a new T.V. collection. You can also stay clear of isolating yourselves from good friends by preparing group activities-- maybe welcome some guests over to your recently hygge-ified house.

Be broad-minded if you're solitary. Don't invest throughout the day glued to your phone, but you can utilize social media sites and dating apps as ways to get and flirt to know others. You never understand that could be waiting on the opposite of your next DM or right swipe.

The Un-Hygge Way: While it's very easy to hibernate and approve of becoming a monk during the cold weather, resist need by learning more about others. On that particular 15th episode of a TELEVISION series binge, reassess pushing play and get yourself available. Sign up with a new club, see a cafe or strike the neighborhood bar to see what's taking place in your community.

Family dinner traditions of Hygge

Hygge Family Dinner Traditions to Start Tonight will certainly offer your ideas on exactly how you can slow down and enjoy having the ability to hang out with your household at a meal.

"Some of one of the most vital conversations I've ever before had occurred at my household's table."-- Bob Ehrlich. Our days can be a whirlwind of activities. So why not take a moment to change the rate of our life by integrating a few concepts to stop and treasure our minutes together with family and friends?

Right here are the Hygge Family Dinner Traditions to Start Tonight:

1) Dine by candlelight.

There's something enchanting regarding sharing a dish by the light of candle lights. You can make this idea a weekly custom or a nightly one.

Nourishing our bodies is a time when we ought to reduce and appreciate the food on our table.

Establish the tone for gratefulness with a little touch of magic.

2) Slow cooker meal.

Instead of working at a hurried speed attempting to get dinner on the table, the simplest solution is to prepare your crockpot before the evening and in the early morning. All you have to do is take it from the refrigerator and plug it in. By the time you're all set to take a seat for supper, your home will certainly smell fantastic and you'll be loosened up from not having to function so hard.

3) Soft songs in the background.

Gorgeous songs set the mood in any setting. We neglect to establish the stage for an ideal night in your home as a simple flick of a button can alter an average night remarkably into a memorable one.

4) Dinner-in-bed.

You know how to do breakfast-in-bed, how around dinner-in-bed? Follow comfortable by wearing your preferred pajamas, get breakfast trays for every person and take pleasure in seeing your favored flick all from the convenience of your bed.

On a specifically demanding day, visit your favorite Chinese dining establishment and order food to-go, and surprise your family members with a dinner-in-bed evening. And all these things will watch the stressful sensations of the day disappear.

You can also assemble a simple charcuterie board full of your favored cheeses, olive oil, marinade olives, balsamic vinegar, figs, nuts, bread, and cold cuts and make that your dinner rather.

5) Natural outing.

Beginning a practice like walking around the block after or prior to supper to expand the moment your family spends together and to take pleasure in the crisp night air.

6) Blessings.

Dinner is an excellent location to understand that we've been blessed. Blessed with good food to consume, honored with friends and family, and honored with a roofing system to sanctuary us.

Every night have your family members consider something in your lives that you are appreciative of and hold that picture in your head. Send a blessing to the person or event that has improved your life.

7) Cooked with love.

Integrate food in your dishes that have meaning. Every bite you take will certainly heat you to your toes.

Show your youngsters how to make a homemade pie from the berries you selected as a family member.

Usage Grandma's recipe for poultry and dumplings for Sunday supper. Keep a flock of poultries and use the eggs in your favorite quiche.

In the summer, head out fishing for your supper.

When you participate in expanding the vegetables and fruits, selecting the apples or berries, dusting or tending the flock off old family member's recipes, and utilizing them in your everyday cooking, the food you eat handles a completely different definition.

8) Dining alfresco.

When you eat your meals outside, it tackles a different rhythm. Even if you're just a few actions away from your home, dining in your very own yard can change a ho-hum evening right into an enchanting one.

It matters not what the season is, each brings its very own presents. Also, winter has its benefits like being toasty warm under heat lights, following your supper with hot cacao, and celebrity gazing.

9) Sporting occasion.

If your family loves sports, plan a laid-back dinner around games you don't want to miss. Your family members will eagerly anticipate hanging out with each other and directing for his/her favorite teams.

Chili and cornbread, homemade poultry soup with crusty sourdough bread, your preferred pizzas with chopped salad, and build-your-own tacos and guacamole and chips are simply a few concepts to select from.

10) Farmers market.

Having links to individuals who generate your food is an extremely hygge method to live. Take your children on an afternoon outing at a local farmers' market so they have the ability to connect with the farmers themselves.

Motivate questions from your youngsters about just how the food is grown, what several of their secrets are, and how a normal day goes.

When you obtain your food residence, have the entire family take part in the production of supper. Assign each person apart while doing so.

11) Fondue night.

Beginning a comfy fire and established supper in front of the fireplace. Spread out a blanket on the flooring or utilize the coffee table as your dining table.

Here are some suggestions of items to dip in your fondue sauces: sirloin, shrimp, or herb-crusted hen in cheese sauce, bread in cheese fondue, pasta-like pasta, or tortellini in alfredo sauce, fit to be tied vegetables in a cheese sauce and fruit for a treat in chocolate fondue.

12) Potluck celebration.

Host a meal celebration once a week or month-to-month at your residence to enjoy the business of your loved ones.

Evening bonfires, parlor game night, card video games, or movie night are just several of the themed concepts you can start with.

13) One good idea.

Every evening go around the table and have each person claim what the highlight of the day was. This maintains every person concentrated on seeking the great moments of each day and providing honor to them.

It could be as simple as getting a fortunate dime, indulging in a delicious bagel with cream cheese, or perhaps a little compliment from a stranger. Nothing is too little.

6. The aspect of nature in Hygge

Hanging out in nature has real health and wellness benefits. Develop the sensation of being outdoors in your indoors by generating natural products like timber, wicker, and even rock.

Live plants-- My online plant wall surface is my outright favorite means to hygge all year. Residence plants include some exhilaration and color and additionally purify indoor air. If you just desire a plant or more, these are my favorite kid-safe interior plants.

Woven baskets-- Baskets in different sizes and shapes around the space are ideal for hiding visual mess like toys or winter months gear.

Free decor-- Get imaginative with intriguing branches, branches, and even rocks from the outdoors and present them in a bowl or vase. Just see to it your kid can't grab and toss the rocks! If you're the smart type, most of these materials can even be made right into artwork!

7. Have some Rituals as part of Hygge

One of the most important facets of hygge is the suggestion of togetherness, which some would argue we do not get much of in our modern-day lives. One way to close that divide and reengage with our youngsters is to take hygge time with each other. Below are some suggestions:

Light a candle together of time-- The process of igniting the candlestick concurrently each day could be assuring. (If in the evening, simply please don't go to sleep prior to you place it out!).

Transform off technology-- Set aside time to transform off gadgets and invest time with each other technology-free. you can also make use of a lockbox or kitchen area safe for our gadgets to secure household time.

Prioritize household dish time-- Food is not only beneficial to the body but also nurtures the soul as well. Pick healthy and balanced dishes (I'll note some listed below) and appreciate a comfy meal with each other. If you can obtain the kids to help prepare it, bonus.

Throw it back-- Think about how households delighted themselves 150 years earlier. Welcome friends over-- Having good friends over is always a good way to get me to put down my to-do listing since I'm focused on being a good host.

Include journaling to the bedtime routine-- Write down the leading 3 points you are grateful for as a household. It doesn't need to be fancy. Yet, a couple of minutes builds a behavior of gratefulness and a feeling of link and health and wellbeing.

Enhance routines you currently have-- Instead of just seeing a film, build a cushion fort and snuggle (or utilize the cover idea from earlier).

Setting aside some uniqueness with each other time doesn't need to be a huge task. Also, one small household routine can make a huge difference in everyone's state of mind and feeling of link. Locate a full listing of our favored household practices here.

Some Cozy bedtime rituals of Hygge

After a stressful day, most of us just fall into bed without decompressing, only to start another busy day the complying with early morning. What if we changed that routine and made going to bed a spiritual period where we nurtured ourselves rather? Comfortable Hygge Bedtime Rituals to Try Tonight may get you started reassessing your night rhythm.

"The key to developing good practices is to make them part of your 'rituals.' I have an early morning routine, afternoon ritual, and Sunday ritual. It's one way to bundle great behaviors into normal times that you set aside to prepare yourself for the life you want. Rituals aid you form routines."-- Lewish Homes

We can transform just how our days unfold as soon as we analyze the way we live our lives and create a deliberate way of living.

Below are the Cozy Hygge Bedtime Rituals to Try:

1) Pick a time for going to bed.

Remain consistent with what time you go to bed and follow this routine even on the weekend breaks. At some point, your body will naturally start unwinding after the habit is regularly coherent.

2) Power down.

Shut off the television, internet, and phone a minimum of one hour before bedtime. You wish to signify to your body that it's time to unwind. By turning off the stimulation early that keeps you awake, you'll have more time to unwind.

3) Candlelight bathroom.

There is absolutely nothing that equals a warm bathroom in my mind for unwinding. I entered into this practice years ago, and whenever I'm having a problem resting, I rise and take a bath. Including candlelight makes this nightly routine even cozier. Simply make sure to finish the bathroom at the very least one hr. before bedtime to make certain ideal rest.

4) Layer your bed.

You spend 1/3 of your life in bed, so make sure it's comfortable and you have the appropriate sheets and blankets. Layers of coverings and great deals of pillows create a comfortable cocoon that will certainly make certain a lovely night's sleep.

5) Goodnight moon.

Make it a routine to go outside, wrapped in a covering, and claim goodnight to the moon. We forget how the most gorgeous points worldwide are totally free.

6) Have some Tea, please!

There's something so remarkable concerning gradually drinking a cozy cup of tea. It's incredibly something so simple is bursting with taste and warms you to the suggestion of your toes. Make sure that you maintain a variety of tea accessible and purchase special seasonal teas when offered.

7) Fairy lights.

There's something so wonderful about fairy lights. Shut off severe lights and sit in the twinkling marvel of your room before dropping off to sleep. Take deep breaths and season in the tranquility.

8) Be thankful.

Every night write in a journal what you are grateful for today. There's a change that happens in all people when we learn to concentrate on what's right with our lives, rather than rewinding the day and thinking of what failed. For more ideas on gratitude.

9) Keep it great.

The ideal temperature to keep your bedroom for the best evening's rest is between 60-67 levels.

10) get lost.

Let a unique publication take you to another time and location. Make it a nighttime ritual to check out before going to bed and provide on your own that quiet time to take your mind off yourself and let your creativity soar.

11) Scented dreams.

Lavender, Jasmine, Lemon, and Bergamot are simply a few of the fragrances that can deepen your sleep. You can have dried out herbs in a bowl or use a diffuser to make envelope your room right into a dreamy state.

12) Snuggle up.

Snuggling with your liked one is the best means to finish the evening. Take the time to cuddle with your pet dog or cat if you do not have a significant various other.

We've reached the end of Cozy Hygge Bedtime Rituals to Try Tonight.

8. Have some Inspiration & Order to High-Traffic Areas.

Hygge is nothing about producing comfortable corners in out-of-the-way locations. Tackling the entranceway was the greatest game-changer for us considering that this is the initial location we see as we get in the home and the place where the many messes get in.

- Use a closed closet rather than open storage to hide the visual mess.
- Hang art or an inspiring quote that has to indicate to you.
- Add a little entryway table with a necessary oil diffuser or a vase of dried blossoms.

9. Have some convenient food to the food selection.

Dishes have constantly been an opportunity for hookup, socializing, and togetherness for every one of human history. These dishes are our preferred healthy and balanced variations of traditional home cooking:

- Mandarin Chicken-- This healthy dish

tastes as good as or far better than other recipes but is much healthier.
- Beef Bourguignon-- This Julia Child-inspired recipe is best for a comfy night.

Cauliflower Beef Stroganoff-- This standard comfort food is made healthier with cauliflower as opposed to egg noodles.

Bean-Free Chili-- This delicious dish only takes a couple of active ingredients, making it a perfect final meal.

Guard's Pie-- as an Irish American, guard's pie is a staple in my family. This set uses healthy cauliflower instead of potatoes.

Meatloaf Cupcakes-- Healthy and enticing to youngsters, this dish is delicious and hygge motivating.

Beef Stroganoff-- A much healthier take-on among my favorite comfort foods from my childhood.

Slow-Cooker Ribs-- Made with honey or molasses as opposed to sugar, this recipe is entire foods only.

Garlic Herb Pot Roast-- Pot roast is one home cooking many people can't live without.

Gingerbread Cookies Recipe-- A real-food means to fill up the air with the smell of cooking and flavors. You can additionally just share warm beverages like a cup of tea or warm delicious chocolate.

10. Have some peace of mind.

Hygge most importantly is a state of mind. It's about reducing and enjoying each minute specifically as it is. While that is never ever easy to do, the more we practice it the simpler it will come to be. Considering that I cannot always lower what I have to do (unless I hand out a child or 2!), I'm attempting to focus on the tiny minutes of peace as they come.

3

PRACTICING THE ART OF HYGGE AT YOUR WORKPLACE

Most offices tend to be filled with the color beige, fluorescent lighting, and uncomfortable chairs. While it likely isn't feasible to remodel your entire work environment, you can start at least. Provide alternative lighting like lamps with bulbs that emit natural light. Otherwise, you can let the employees bring their own if they have a preference. Replace stiff chairs with more comfortable and ergonomic alternatives— maybe even some with cozy cushions.

For those who have their own space, encourage them to decorate it to their liking. One thing that everyone seems to agree on is that- candles carry the highest degree of the hygge philosophy. Most corporate offices don't permit real candles, but some great battery-operated candles mimic real flames.

Consider offering them as a small token of hygge to your employees.

In Denmark, they go as far as having colorful hygge socks that employees slip into as they enter the office.

We don't go that far here at Beekeeper, but for some of our cold, foggy San Francisco days, it doesn't sound like a bad idea!

Hygge is all about an experience and an atmosphere, instead than about points. It concerns being with the individuals we like. A feeling of home.

Hygge is seemed to be proper at that moment, as I felt a wind blowing via my windows and scented the rejuvenating aroma of my burning "Storm Watch" candle. My father was outside while my mom planted her home window boxes in the front backyard. I could easily recognize then that this is what hygge is about-- the little things that make your heart full.

It's simple to maintain this attitude of comfort, well- being and safety when you're home, surrounded by fresh coffee and giggling, unclear socks and Netflix, homemade cookies, and brighter blossoms. However, the office is typically where one needs to hygge the most. You don't want to turn up to a nine-hour shift moping and feeling drowsy from lack of interest. You intend to welcome your co-workers with kindness and exhilaration for the day in advance.

Exercising hygge can assist lower anxiety, anxiety. In the Foundation's latest psychological health and drug abuse study record, these allow difficulties affecting efficiency, medical care expenses, and absenteeism for companies. Over fifty percent (57%) of workers are influenced by stress and anxiety, 63% by clinical depression, and 93% by tension.

You invest a minimum of 8 hours a day at the workplace. For some it's even more, for the lucky few, it's less. If you live in North America, for certain months of the year, you get up in the dark to visit your workplaces and return home in the dark.

That's a great deal of dark.

So what would certainly take place if you applied the Danish concept of happiness to your everyday job life?

Do you understand Hygge?

Would certainly your co-workers assume you're insane if you rested in the middle of the afternoon? What would your manager say if you started lighting candles everywhere? Well, perhaps candles would not work.

Utilizing the power of hygge to bring coziness and satisfaction into your life isn't just limited to home and family. Creating a comfy place to function by embracing hygge in very simple means can take the rough edges of your workplace cubicle. It can develop a small hygge neighborhood of work friends, and infuse a little hygge house decoration.

But I think you can reach that cozy hygge area at the workplace, by including a few small things, and some basic methods right into your job day. This publication will assist you to develop a better workspace and contribute to a positive job community. Many thanks for sticking with me!

Making your workplace extra hygge is an exceptional means to enhance staff member contentment levels and involvement.

Ways to make your workplace more hygge:

- The view of Hygge from a work environment

Many workplaces often tend to be loaded with shade beige, fluorescent lighting, and unpleasant chairs. While isn't practical to renovate your whole workplace, you can begin with tiny steps at least. Supply alternative lights like lamps with bulbs that send out natural light, or allow employees to bring their own if they have a choice. Replace tight chairs with even more comfortable and ergonomic choices--maybe even some with comfortable paddings.

One point that every person seems to concur on is that candles bring the greatest degree of the hygge philosophy. Think about providing them as a little token of hygge to your staff members.

In Denmark, they reach having colorful hygge socks that employees slip into as they go into the workplace. We do not go that far here at Beekeeper, but for several of our cool, clouded San Francisco days, it doesn't sound like a negative concept!

- Update your work desk

Some obvious adjustments can make your very own area feel cozier, presuming they do not damage the fire code and don't check off your cubemates:

Add a lamp with an incandescent light bulb to counteract the above fluorescents and heaven light coming from your screen.

Maintain a soft scarf or coat on the back of your chair to combat awesome office temps and tight chairs. Even better, placed that scarf/jacket on your lap as a makeshift covering.

Change footwear (or do not). I would venture a guess that nobody would notice if you "neglected" to change out of your commuting sneakers/winter boots.

Certain, I function for NPR, however, I cannot listen to music, radio, or podcasts and focus on the layout at the same time (oh, the irony). Coworkers also like white noise that appears like a coffee store.

- Look for a comfortable area

Try some alternating rooms for a modification of scene if you have a helpful workplace with a trust that you'll function even when you're not at your desk.

Discover or make a space that feels more intimate if your workplace is open-concept and sizable. Drag a comfortable chair alongside a cabinet. You can also see if there's a tiny area or workplace where you might function once in a while.

Change meeting areas. Assemble the team in the common location or cafe if you're not dependent on meeting room innovation. Find smaller-sized tables and rest closer to your coworkers.

- Use the art of Hygge in your interaction style.

To a more thoughtful degree, hygge embodies consistency and togetherness which go together. This aesthetic art will let you not see your work as a place for competitors, however as an area to be modest and work as a team to complete goals.

Internal communication style that encourages structure partnerships with your colleagues. Celebrate tiny or large, work or individual successes in the work environment and acknowledge those that exceed and beyond for the organization. See exactly how "sentiment analysis" can additionally be integrated into your inner interaction method.

- Get used to making little conversations a normal point

Personal link is a facet of hygge that I both need and concern. I'm an autist that believes other individuals are interesting, so I often wish to chat-- yet feel nervous about it.

Schedule quick regular check-ins with your favorite colleagues to see if you remain to link, even when points get busy. These individuals are your gut check/cheerleader/commiserator.

For a coworker, you would certainly like to understand better, welcome them to a 30-minute one-on-one. This can be a fast coffee, Skype conversation, or lunchroom catch-up. You don't require a program, yet

do take into consideration a few things to keep up the conversation.

Don't ignore colleagues that work remotely! They may require aid production and preserving personal links, so be a pal and reach out.

- Avoid multitasking.

A big part of hygge is residing in the minute, which is difficult if you're constantly multitasking. Allows to face it-- we're all guilty of trying to do too many things at once. Exactly how typically do you find coworkers (and yourself) analyzing emails while joining a conference call, or paying attention to a coworker's tale while submitting reports?

Hygge recommends not multitasking at all and bearing in mind one task. Since research studies reveal that, multitasking is pricey and doesn't work, which is a great ideology. Advise your workers to shut off notices that don't apply to them and permit them to take short breaks to kick back and refocus.

- Get some extra daytime

You may like the extra sunlight in the morning, or despise commuting home in the dark. But November implies the end of Daylight Saving Time, and we are

persevered till the spring. We can avoid "falling back" right into funk by setting more time aside for daytime.

I recognize everyone claims to leave your desk at lunch, and I desire I took their guidance. I am much more likely to walk away during that hour if I have a task, so think up a few little jobs you can do near the office that will obtain you outside.

Take into consideration little changes to your commute to obtain a little daylight. Leave the train one stop earlier. Stroll to the second-closest bus quit. Park just a little more away.

Take smoke breaks. No, I'm kidding! However,

if your day is adaptable, consider strolling to grab a coffee or merely do a lap around the block.

- Carry a mug with you from your home

Having a warm drink to sip, even on summer days, is calming, and caffeine is a proven way to boost your power and maintain concentration on your tasks.

"Take time to enjoy a mug of coffee with a colleague and discuss non-work-related topics. "Use a coffee cup that you enjoy in the office."

Drinking out of your preferred mug resembles having a piece of residence with you. Do not hesitate to get up from time to time for a refill, giving your brain a break from mundane tasks.

- Exercise more of hygge during lunch breaks.

A lot of people do not take a complete lunch break. Research shows that taking a break every hour improves productivity, yet several managers seem aggravated when their group tries to enjoy their lunch break.

If personnel participants have a peaceful place to appreciate their short time away from work, it's even a lot handier. However, if that's impossible, supplying staff members with the right products to enjoy a nice dish can help. Clean home appliances and actual tools can make a big distinction in the group's frame of mind and can boost the hygge of your work environment

- Spend lunch outside or take that time to take a break

When you take your lunch break, really pause. Don't check e-mail, plan your following assignment, or stare at your computer while eating the PB and J you loaded.

If it's nice outside, receive some clean air. Depending on where you work, walk the block to the nearby delicatessens or appreciate your jam-packed lunch on a bench at the park. Whatever the situation, getting outdoors will certainly assist you to take a break for a while, and exploring the area might raise your spirits.

- Have a sense of coziness at your workspace

Consistently try to accommodate some private things decorating your room, ranging from pictures of your member of the family to a bouquet of tulips you bought at the farmer's market. Bring cord lights to drape around your cubicle or maintain plenty of tea on hand and vintage publications stacked around your work desk. Do not be afraid to stray from the norm (within your business's plans, obviously).

- Undertake the following actions to make your job area cozy

Lovely plants make it comfortable and we like the charm of succulents. They are so easy to take care of, can be found in many fascinating designs and stunning shades of environment-friendly. Or stop at the grocers or fruit depends on your method to choose and work up a big bouquet of fresh-cut flowers.

Set up a Tea and Coffee station on your own and associates to participate in. You can grab some clear glass jars at the neighborhood buck store, grab a tea infuser, a tiny French press, and some cute cups and in your room tray, and set up your very own hot beverage room. Take your tea or coffee break at the same time each day, so that folks know they can wander over to your work area at the same time and take pleasure in some hygge tea!

Sweaters and coverings can be layered over the rear of your chair, or piled on a cupboard. I love my comfy covering serape that the children provided to me last Christmas. Offices are generally also cold or also warm, so be comfortable having the ability to layer up or down.

When a month organizes a team to bring in their

preferred dishes for lunch. You can bring quiet paper napkins and paper plates, and ask everybody to bring their very own recipes and flatware.

- Move around and take breaks from time to time

Produce a playlist of your favorites. Or enroll in Audible! Such a remarkable resource and you get two free downloads when you join.

Pictures, fresh flowers and art prints-One of the simplest means to include some hygge at the office are to bring in some household images and cheer up your office with some charming art prints.

Random acts of kindness-- is there somebody brand- new that could use a good friend? Or perhaps you understand someone who is having a problem with elder treatment or balancing childcare and work. Think of small things that you could do to lighten their tons.

Embellish your office at Easter, St. Patrick's Day, or the 4th of July! Buck stores like Dollar Tree are excellent locations to get enjoyable designs.

I've taken this action further and asked to have the light bulbs gotten rid of from the fixture over my dice. That way I remove the severe glow from both the illumination and the computer screen, decreasing the effect on my eyes.

- Hold a potluck with your people

You can enjoy hygge in a comfortable solitude, another way to make this practice your own is to spend time cherishing loved ones. Once you've equipped your home with everything regarding hygge, nothing is sweeter than sharing it with your friends and family. Invite them over for an intimate gathering with comforting food and drink. Refill coffee, tea, and other warm beverages. Wrap up in cozy blankets on comfortable pillows. Relish the conversation and laughter that will inevitably flow.

Home cooking is the source of all things that hygge can offer you. and what much better method to relish home-cooked dishes than with your work buddies at hand taste- testing one another's meals?

Depending On to Jessica Joelle Alexander, co-author of "The Danish Technique of Parenting" and co-creator of "The Danish Way" blog site, friendly events entailing food are a Danish sensation.

"The suggestion is that eating together promotes time to hygge with your workers," Alexander claimed. "[It's] a location where you can connect and be in the minute and delight in being together," Wiking suggests workers arrange a dinner day as opposed to bringing lunch for themselves.

"When everybody shares, everyone obtains hygge," he claimed.

Carry out various arbitrary acts of compassion for your associates

Whether it's delivering a box of doughnuts to the work environment or just using an approval to an affiliate, you can easily transform a person's entire day (and your very own) around by being kind.

"Social aid carries out help manage tension and stress," declared Iben Sandahl, Alexander's co-author in addition to co-creator of "The Danish Way." According to Sandahl, identifying our company have people who recognize us creates our company even more durable.

"Being vulnerable with individual authorizations a huge circulation of the stress and anxiety and stress our expert's lug, aiding to receive it off our spines," Sandahl explained.

Appreciate and uphold the art of synergy

Sandahl stated team spirit is part of Danish society. From childhood years, Danish people operate in groups and are taught to look for and/or offer help in the face of misfortune. They are encouraged to remain certain despite their weaknesses and simpleness regardless of their toughness.

"This spirit of teamwork and collaboration is seen in all facets of Danish life-- from the classroom to the office to family life," stated Sandahl. "Seeing the family members as a team cultivates a deep feeling of belonging. The same spirit [is something] you can take into the conference room also."

Sandahl recommends arranging much more team-building activities to encourage working together, from scavenger hunts to tournaments.

Gove and van Renswoude noted that as soon as individuals understand hygge, they unexpectedly recognize all the small, unique moments in their lives.

"Being mindful of these moments enables you to produce even more of them," they said. "A hygge way of living is not about excellence yet concerning reducing to enjoy and be content in also the smallest of moments."

- Seasonal celebrations of Hygge at work.

Every period comes birthing gifts. Ensure you commemorate those offerings by bringing a few of the bounties to your work environment.

Spring season:

Set up tulips or daffodils in a vase.

Strawberries, a fresh spinach salad, or seasoned asparagus, could be added to your lunch box.

- Summer:

Roses floating in a recipe of water on top of your work desk would certainly be calming and gorgeous.

Cherry pie or peach cobbler would make any person delighted at lunch.

- Fall:

Dahlias and Gerbera's sissies would certainly brighten up any workplace.

Pieces of apples and sugar dip or heating a pleasant potato with loads of butter and brown sugar seem like they would hit the spot.

- Winter:

Forced paperwhites or a Christmas cactus are just sensational. Persimmons and a kale salad are simply several of the suggestions for a tasty winter lunch.

Comfy accents for hygge at work.

You can soften up difficult and tougher areas by adding some simple components to your workplace. And these simple but aesthetic additions have no less credibility to win your mind.

Several niches you can include for this aesthetic addition are mounted artwork, a bud vase with a solitary flower or generate an arrangement of flowers each week, LED candles flickering throughout the day, a salt lamp such as this one that will help relieve your anxiety, family pictures, a wall surface calendar with photos you like, a cozy rug under your work desk, slippers to maintain your feet snug, a nice paperweight, a unique mouse pad, a captivating display saver, a fortunate bamboo plant, fairy lights strung up, gently-played gorgeous songs, a picture of yourself when you were young, a great delicious chocolate bar, face spritz, jar of desserts, a little teddy bear or a really felt fox, a pillow for your chair, baskets to hold your products, little shelves to hold trinkets, hang a tiny patchwork, a poster of where you intend to take a trip to, a string of butterflies, images of your yard, list of what you're happy for, inspiring phrases, your favorite hand lotion, a vital oil diffuser and heart notes are simply several of the important things you can include.

4

MAKING A BACKYARD GARDEN
THROUGH THE ART OF HYGGE

The surest way to make your garden feel more Hygge is to bring some of the insides out by creating an Outdoor Living Area. It all starts with a comfy outdoor lounge setting. Create an Outdoor Dining Area. Outdoor Cinema. Star or Sun Gazing. Wine & Pizza Night. Candle Light. Fairy Lights. Pretty Pot Plants.

It's time to make your residence feel like a cozy area to be, even in the summer season! Changing your yard right into an enchanting location where you can reenergize is the ideal way to provide on your own an existing that goes on giving. Why purchase points that will not bring you happiness daily?

Producing a hygge life suggests putting in the time to create an environment that induces you to unwind and delight in what life needs to offer.

Some astonishing illumination.

You understand stringing fairy lights in your home change it right into a relaxing nook. So why not enhance your yard with some charming lights that will immediately calm your spirit?

Look exactly how gorgeous these lights are strung together. I can feel the stress leave your shoulders just looking at them.

Feathered pals.

I like taking place garden scenic tours. Seeing just how others change their spaces into something that makes everyone want to unite at their house makes me smile.

The yard that sticks out in my mind was thought out so every part of it had a stamp of personality. The one thread that wove all the components with each other was the proprietor's love for birds. They made her satisfied.

Her yard was a place where she can return the present of all the happiness they offered her and make them delighted. Happy they were, let me tell you. The reason this yard sticks out so much in my mind was not just for its appeal. However, as a result of how many birds there were appreciating their little paradise.

Her birdbaths offered moving fresh water and security from killers. She had various bird feeders around the building to draw in a variety of various kinds of birds. No pesticides were made use of in the garden and there was little lawn in the yard--primarily winding pathways with yard beds all over.

Favored fruit.

What's your favorite fruit? Is it lemons? Just how around some berries like raspberries, blueberries, cranberries, tayberries, or strawberries? Do grapes make you drool simply considering them?

Plant your own bush, tree, or plants to make certain you have an ample supply of your preferred fruit all summer long.

A themed garden through Hygge.

Why have a regular garden, when you can produce a themed one that will bring a smile to your face whenever you see it?

Several of the suggestions you may wish to consider can be a fairy garden, butterfly yard, moonlight garden, increased yard, pizza yard, cut blossom garden, fragrant yard, friendship yard, Shakespeare garden, or a tea yard are simply a few of the possibilities.

Relaxing fire.

Sectioning off a part of your backyard for a fire pit is the ideal means to relax in the evening and spending quality time with your friends and family. You can even make your evening dish in it and not heat up your house with the oven. Aluminum foil package dishes are both fun and delicious and easy to do.

Easy chair.

Choose a comfy lounge chair for evening stargazing. There's no demand to strain your neck from a chair when you can lay back and take in the beautiful night sky.

The very best time to do stargazing is in August when the Perseids meteor shower takes place. In 2018 the very best days to watch are August 11-13th.

Alfresco dining.

There's no need of staying indoors eating your dishes on a summer day. As quickly as the weather condition starts to heat up, adapt your strategy to offer all your food on an outdoor table and chairs.

Location blossoms in your yard in mason containers on the table to perk things up and see to it your chairs have padding. So they are comfortable for both on your own and friends and family. Part of the hygge way of life is to spend high quality with your liked ones and eating a dish outside together.

Decorative touches.

Adding unique touches to your gardens like concrete sculptures, arbors, mirrors, and iron garden gateways will certainly provide your exterior area a more comfortable atmosphere. You intend to give your yard a "lived-in" look, so you feel comfy the very moment you tip outside.

Exactly how around adding a touch of whimsy to make you smile?

Organic delight.

There's something great about the aroma of herbs that enliven our wellness. The fantastic thing about having lots of natural herbs in your backyard is that they do not use up much space. Not only do they scent terrific, but also you can save some cash by not

having to get them in the food store for your food preparation.

You can likewise preserve them for the winter season so you can appreciate them throughout the year.

Swing.

Isn't seeing a solitary swing in a garden enchanting? Consider how simple it is to add one to your heaven. Ask yourself why you have not done it up before?

It's an easy step in adding that special nod to the past back right into your life.

Imaginative side.

How about making something unique for your yard utilizing your creative abilities? Mosaics are the ideal method to include beauty and beauty to any type of yard.

Mosaics can be utilized to add accents to walls, sculptures, or perhaps stepping-stones.

Gazebo.

A gazebo includes beauty that is unequaled in my eyes. Tactically putting your gazebo in the appropriate place is the best means to invest a day enjoying your life. Thus, you can be able to appreciate all the bounty your backyard needs to supply too!

Enchanting touches.

You might not want to make an entire fairy garden of your yard. However, what about including only a touch of fantasy with either a fairy pot? Or, a tree that has a fairy door affixed to the trunk and even a wood toadstool or two? How about expanding a few pots of four-leaf clovers to include in your luck?

Yard video games.

Board games aren't the only method you can challenge your loved ones to a little competition. Make sure you have a selection of lawn games like croquet, backyard bowling, a ring toss, horseshoes, or tennis for some old-fashioned enjoyable

Winding course.

There's something concerning a winding course in a yard that's so unique. I change the path to my front door to one that winds as opposed to going straight because it's intended to bring all the best.

5
WHY DANISH PEOPLE ARE AMONG THE HAPPIEST PEOPLE

The people of Denmark are the happiest in the world according to the latest scientific. The media's attention to this issue has led the Danish people to talk about it. If you asked the reason for the happiness and satisfaction with the life of Danish people three years ago, they would probably have looked at you in a glimpse of what this question is.

But today, in response to such a question, most Danes are likely to offer many reasons for their happiness with and satisfaction. It took many years for the Danish people to believe that they are the happiest people in the world. In the past, many people in the world thought that the lives of the people of the northern European region were very uneasy. For an instance, Denmark was a country with high suicide and depression rates.

Denmark is well-known for being the best "hap-

Hygge

piest country around the world." Its stereotype is that of semi-socialist heaven where medical care is completely free of charge. Students are paid by the federal authorities to see college. In addition to the nationwide pastime is snuggling before a howling fire along with a glass of red wine and an excellent manual.

In 2017, Denmark was slammed from the scratch spot in the World Joy Record through neighboring Norway. Nonetheless, Danish people have placed No. 1 in happiness for 3 of recent 5 years.

Nordic countries have in fact ruled the planet happiness positions looking at that the initial Planet Joy Document came out in 2012. All the five Nordic countries (Denmark, Finland, Iceland, Norway, and Sweden) rated in the leading 10 based upon 6 essential standards: freedom, generosity, wellness, social support, earnings, and trustworthy administration. Although GDP is higher in the United States than all Nordic countries, Americans are still just the 14th happiest people on earth.

So why precisely are those LEGO-playing, pastry-eating Danish people winning the joy race? We reached out to Helen Russell, writer of 'The Year of Living Danishly: Uncovering the Secrets of the World's Happiest Country', to obtain the scoop from a long-lasting Londoner who moved to Denmark five years ago and dropped all of a sudden for its calm, comfort-loving society. Here are

Russell's 5 reasons Danish people are happier than you.

In studies, 79 percent of Danish people state they count on the bulk of individuals. I don't trust 79 percent of my instant house," jokes Russell that moved coming from Greater London to Denmark in 2013 when her husband got a task-- where else?

Denmark's small population (far fewer than 6 thousand) and cultural agreement possess one thing to perform along with it. However, the Danish sense of the matter is extensive, coming from next-door neighbors to authorities. Russell specifies most Danish people do not protect their automobiles and vehicle doors or even frontal doors. Depend on isn't an innate Danish quality, Russell admits. In "The Year of Residing Danishly," Russell spoke with political analyst Peter Thisted Dinesen coming from Copenhagen College. It positioned for the likewise immigrants from "low-trust" nations that are educated in Denmark promptly tackle Danish levels of a trust fund.

The Danish welfare and performance

People from Danish pay for a few of the greatest earnings tax obligation rates worldwide, forty-five percent (45%) for regular Danish annual earnings of $43,000 and 52 percent for those that make greater than $67,000. In exchange for handing over half their earnings, every Dane receives cost-free wellness treatment, complimentary K-college education (pupils are paid $900 a month), extremely subsidized youngster care, and charitable unemployment advantages. According to relative studies, every 9 out of 10 Danish people claim that they gladly pay their inflated tax obligations.

"The reason behind the high level of assistance for the well-being state in Denmark is the understanding of the fact that the well-being model turns our collective wide range right into health," creates Meik Wiking, primary executive officer of Denmark's Happiness Research Institute. "We are not paying tax obligations.

If you lose a job in Denmark, it's not always a large offer. Thanks to something called the "flexicurity model," companies in Denmark have a whole lot even more freedom to fire staff members. It's because there are federal government programs to re-train workers and much better position them for the task market.

Denmark also has among the most charitable retired life systems on the planet, attending to the 65-plus populace with a combination of a state-funded pension plan and private, employer-funded pension plan programs. Again, when you're not constantly bothered with just how you're going to manage your retired life, you're most likely to feel much less nervous and much more secure. In other words, happier.

Danish people Work Less and Spend More Time with Their Families

"Work-life balance" in Denmark isn't just a Human Resources buzzword, rather, it's a lifestyle. Danish employees placed in the second-fewest hrs. Of all Organization for Economic Cooperation and Development (OECD) countries at 1,412 hours a year. If Danish people worked all 52 weeks a year, that would average bent on just 27 hrs. A week, but because most Danish companies use at least 5 weeks of the paid trip, Russell says that the real number is closer to 33 hours a week. Still, 33 hours a week?

"As a family, we are gently annoyed if my hubby does not get the house up until 5:30 p.m.," states Russell, who gets on maternity leave with twin 3-month-olds. "In London, we hardly saw each other."

On the subject of adult leaves, Denmark once more has among one of the most generous policies on the planet. The government calls for all companies to offer up to 52 weeks of leave, for either mother or dad. And, the state gives financial assistance for as much as 32 weeks.

For every one of the time off that Danish workers take, economic performance does not appear to suffer. According to OECD computations of labor performance (GDP per hour worked), Denmark rates well above bigger economic climates like Germany, Japan, and the United States. Russell credit ratings a various work environment cultures.

Denmark is the ultimate "hygge headquarter" in a sense. They also have a word for it: 'hjemmehygge' (house hygge). It may describe the Danish obsession with a great layout.

They also have one of the most living spaces per capita in Europe

"There's this concept that you work hard, obtain the job done and after that go residence. Danish people do not lose time at the office on Facebook," Russell claims. "You're additionally relied on by your employer to do an excellent task, so you have the overall flexibility to work from residence or choose your very own schedule."

"In all the work I have done within the field of a joy research study. This is the point I am surest concerning: the very best forecaster of whether we enjoy it or not is our social connections.

Journalist Cathy Strongman, that moved from London to Copenhagen and who wrote in The Guardian: "Work later than 5:30 and the workplace is a morgue. Operate at the weekend and the Danish people think you are mad. The idea is that households have time to play and consume with each other at the end of the day, each day."

The Danish people do not boast

There's a word-of-mouth law in Danish society phoned Janteloven or "Jante's legislation", based upon a preferred ridiculing story from the 1930s.

The spirit of Janteloven is "do not act like you're better, smarter or richer than any person else."

Janteloven has shed some of its grip in cosmopolitan Copenhagen. Russell says, "it's still very much lived by ordinary Danish people" (you might also say that being "typical" is the goal).

Every person is equivalent," claims Russell, including that you don't see even wealthy Danish people living or driving fancy automobiles in extravagant residences. "People also dress rather informal; I haven't seen a connection in years."

Not only are there fewer exterior indicators of success or battle, but failing in Denmark isn't a four-letter word, Russell states. Since Danish people afford such a strong safety net, there isn't as much monetary threat in failure. So, the individuals feel free to attempt new points. If it doesn't work out, no large loss.

The Danish people live a Hygge lifestyle

To recognize what makes Danish people better and why they're so darn delighted, you have to recognize hygge. Russell says that hygge is more than simply crackling timber fires and full-body pajamas, it's anything that brings you deep, soul-warming pleasure.

Russell claims that Danish people are "bemused and staggered" that hygge has come to be a fashionable self-help fad. A quick search on Amazon reveals more than a dozen hygge-themed books assuring to expose the Danish key to happiness. Seems like the ideal read for that barking fire.

Food and drinks

"Sweets are hyggelige. Cake is hyggeligt. Coffee or warm delicious chocolate is hyggeligt, as well. Carrot sticks, not a lot," Wiking states.

He believes that the high degree of coffee, confectionery, and meat intake in Denmark is straight connected to hygge.

"Hygge is about being kind to on your own-- giving on your own a reward, and offering on your own, and each other, a break from the demands of healthy living," he claims.

Wiking's compatriots appear to agree: The average Dane consumes 3 kilos of bacon a year.

Christmas

Christmas is one of the most hyggelig parts of the year. "Even though it is feasible to hygge throughout the year, just yearly is hygge the utmost goal of a whole month," he says. Xmas traditions in Denmark do not differ from those in the UK or the United States. Yet, the difference is that "a Danish Christmas will certainly always be planned, thought of, and examined in relation to the idea of hygge." There is also a word for it-- julehygge (Christmas-hygge).

Lighting

From its iconic lampshades to the staggeringly prevalent use of candle lights. Denmark is a country obsessed with illumination. The Happiness Research Institute's researches reveal that, 85% of individuals connect hygge with candles; 28% of Danish people light candles every day.

Wiking quotes the American ambassador to Denmark, who states candles develop "a sort of emotional happiness, an emotional coziness."

6

ACHIEVING PERSONAL AND HOUSEHOLD HARMONY THROUGH THE HYGGE LIFESTYLE

For most of my life, I've sought consistency. What is the definition of life? When is a life worthwhile of being lived?

In the previous couple of years, I've gathered some crucial life insights-- my life concepts. As a component of my individual transformation, growing over time (some might call it obtaining older, and hopefully smarter), moving with the quadrants, transforming from terrified to healthy once more, I have actually discovered these principles have helped me to get energized.

What can moms and dads do to bring some tranquility to the household? A brand-new study reveals that when moms and dads try to settle their teens' disputes, in reality, they may develop more troubles between the kids. A brand-new study reveals attempting to produce consistency with more "family time" is ideal.

The method parents can best advertise positive, low-conflict partnerships is to be proactive - Don't punish them; do not endanger them. It's not going to help at this moment. Discover points you can do with them that you can take pleasure in and they can delight in. You can have favorable experiences, and it will make them hesitate before they pester and strike each other."

You will have no question to find various principles. Check out with mine, make use of what jobs for you, make a decision which ones you would like to follow.

In their study, released in the August issue of the Journal of Marriage and the Family, researchers interacted with moms, dads, and teenagers in 185 white, functioning, middle-class households. Each family had 2 youngsters; firstborns averaged age 15 and their siblings averaged 13.5 years old.

"Those that had the most effective brother or sister connections," she says, "were those family members who spent time with each other simply doing ordinary points like having dishes and watching TV". The whole family members really did not have to be with each other. It had been great if one sibling was with a minimum of among their parents. "Our conjecture was that it's unlikely that children would be willing to hang around with their parents or brother or sisters unless they have a fairly cozy, cohesive family in the first place," McHale says.

They also discovered that, when conflict developed between the youngsters, no quantity of adult intervention assisted. In fact, "moms and dads' efforts to settle those conflicts might generate even more negativity in the brother or sister partnership," says McHale.

"One theory is that parents must remain out of it, that the reason children fight is to get parents' attention. Moms and dads can make children fight more by just how they respond. Parents who are punitive, extreme, and intimidating make youngster's combat more often."

Some moms and dads attempted mentoring kids on how to exercise troubles, which some researchers have revealed are effective in younger kids, McHale states. Nevertheless, her study revealed training to be ineffective with teenagers. "By the time you reach teenage years, if you're still training your children, you need to have some quite intractable brother or sister connection issues.

"Mothers had a tendency to react to conflict by overlooking it, allowing kids to function it out by themselves. The exception: when households had older kids and younger children.

Wanting to shield the child is "not a problem," claims McHale. Lessons in compassion and problem resolution should have begun much earlier. Parents "should have been working through youth with training approaches, locating points your kids have in common and spending time with them. You cannot start with a really poor brother or sister relationship in adolescence and fix it."

"Preschool and early school-age years are when moms and dads ought to hang around discussing exactly how one child feels when the various other one acts a certain means, helping them see other perspectives, training dispute resolution methods. These are necessary points to do in younger children. Our data recommends that if you're simply beginning that in teenage years, you might be far too late; you've actually missed out on an essential chance," she stated.

"I do not like at fault parents," states McHale. "I think parents have a lot of needs on them today. As the moms and dads of youngsters in middle childhood years, I can tell you, there is all sort of pressure to obtain children outside of the home, to football, ballet, and language lessons, and art lessons ... however, they're not created to construct family relationships. Equilibrium is key. The bottom line is, you can't have all of it."

When kids remain in problem, moms and dads need to step back and remember that their children are maturing, Nadine Kaslow, Ph.D., tells WebMD. "How a parent gets associated with their children's conflict does depend on the age of the kid. Kaslow is a teacher and principal psychologist in the psychology and behavioral sciences at Emory University School of Medicine in Atlanta.

"Don't obtain entailed in every little detail with your teens", claims Kaslow. "For regular brother or sister dispute, nonnative involvement yet awareness from a distance ... you do not desire to be so uninvolved that you have no concept what's going on, but you don't require to be actively included. If the conflict is a lot more significant, you might require to interfere".

The secret behind Family Harmony through Hygge lifestyle

Being consistent-- setting restrictions for your child and adhering to them-- is a tried and tested way to influence teamwork, compassion, good manners, etc. We've got methods to assist you to persevere.

My daddy cooked an uncommon pasta, hen, and veggie mixture when we were on vacation with my moms and dad. My 6-year-old, sister, looked at it and stated, No, she'll be great," I claimed. She commonly possesses the alternative in between consuming what

I have actually prepared or consuming definitely nothing at all, which guideline had really been actually working exceptionally for our team.

My daddy forgot me and went back into the

kitchen space. He came back with barbequed cheese.

Certainly, not would like to create waves, I informed on my own, "Our team performs the trip. Permit it to go." I permit it to go night after night. As he created a unique dish after more than two weeks later in the house, I made chicken and corn on the cob, which Kaarina had constantly liked. That night, nevertheless, she yawped, "I despise corn on the cob!"

"You do not have to eat it," I responded smoothly. "You recognize the rule. You can eat this or consume absolutely nothing. It's your choice."

If I'd simply stuck to our typical food policy on getaway and firmly told my mild-mannered dad not to cook Kaarina various meals, I'm certain her tantrum would have been prevented. "If you offer in one out of ten times, it's worse than giving in every time," claims Kelly McGonagall, Ph.D., writer of The Willpower Instinct and a speaker at Stanford University. Inconsistent parenting-- applying policies, regimens, and repercussions often but not always. She encourages youngsters to do specifically what we don't want them to do: gripe, grumble, negotiate, question our judgment, and ignore us.

Naturally, being flawlessly consistent is less complicated said than done. As an example, even if you have a "half an hour of TV a day" policy, you could damage it when you're on the phone and require your youngsters to be quiet. Or, like me, you could anticipate your children to adhere to a rule that you do not constantly follow yourself. Kaarina isn't enabled to say the word silly at school and yet I usually claim it in the house. Specifically, when I'm referring to our brand-new canine that's just damaged another thing in the house.

Being a foreseeable mom and dad needs to be your best objective. "This allows youngsters to recognize that they have a choice: They can pay attention to you or they can deal with the consequences," says Patti Cancellier, Education and Learning planner for the Parent Encouragement Program in Kensington, Maryland. To assist you to stay solid and motivate fantastic behavior, think about these typical reasons that parents cave.

Shame

Your youngster gripes for sweet on the checkout line. "You feel uncomfortable and nervous and you simply want that feeling to go away," claims Dr. McGonagall. You get the candy, and your kid turns off the rips.

The Solution

Evaluate the temporary reward of providing her what she desires (ending the disaster, buying your grocery stores in tranquility) against the long-lasting cost of providing in (future temper tantrums that are more mortifying). This will certainly activate your prefrontal cortex-- the self-control facility of the mind-- and make the tough job of parenting really feel much easier, says Dr. McGonagall. With your brand-new willpower, you could ditch the groceries and take your youngster straight to the vehicle.

Faulty Reasoning

When we were on our trip with my parents, this was my error. I believed, "Two weeks of unhealthy eating isn't going to mess this child up for life. Why trouble my dad regarding this?" Maybe you've come to a comparable final thought. However, it was "What's the injury in five even more mins of computer game?" or "One late evening isn't a big deal." Except it is a big deal. If you flex the regulations this time, you are just providing your child much more power following time-- power that you can be sure he will certainly make use of versus you with a remark like, "You let me stay up last evening. Why cannot I keep up later on this evening?"

These are a few other types of faulty reasoning: My kid really did not do what I said, so I should ask once again. And once more. And once more, even more loudly. "As opposed to getting your youngster's attention, this encourages him to tune you out," claims Cancellier. He thinks, "I know my mother isn't most likely to do anything regarding this until she asks me the 6th time and she's very angry." He waits for the sixth inquiry. I desire my child to cooperate, so I'll threaten the worst possible penalty I can think of and hope that he behaves so I don't need to actually penalize him. If you don't follow up with this mega-consequence, nevertheless, your kid will discover that you do not truly mean what you say. And he's probably most likely to rebel, even more," claims family member's therapist Hal Runkel, author of Scream Free Parenting.

The Solution

Only ask your kid as soon as, stand beside him with a hand on his back and a smile on your face, and wait, suggests Cancellier. If he's offering you a difficult time concerning a choice you've made, reiterate your placement and shift his focus away from what he desires today-- more TELEVISION time or potato chips to something he wants in the future.

You could say, "You're not likely to have even more TV currently, yet if you go to bed without difficulty, you can have TELEVISION once more tomorrow."

Following time you can take it method for 10. "If you advise him that you'll take it away for three minutes and follow with, next time he'll assume, 'I much better pay attention because she's actually going to do it,'" says Runkel.

Interruption

You're on the phone and your child asks you for a cookie. You state, "Whatever, honey," and hand her the plan so she can take one herself. You perform not presume concerning it when again until later on when you discover the unfilled container and a number of crumbs on her space floor. Existed?

"Being sidetracked damages our resolve in addition to degrading our moments, inducing our company to fail to remember the guidelines, and results in our company's linking to be normal around," says Runkel. This happens whenever our team is actually trying to do two factors all at once, aside from when our team is actually starving, stressed, or even remainder robbed.

The Solution

"You require to become rested to be a consistent parent, therefore be just as meticulous about your own bedtime as you have to do with your child's. Also, take a difficult one, considering your timetable and your family members' timetable, too," suggests Susan Newman, Ph.D., writer of The Book of No: '250 Ways to Say It-- and Mean It'. If they make you really feel anxious and hurried, consider reducing back on playgroups or extracurricular tasks. Advise yourself that not every e-mail or message needs to be addressed today. The house does not need to be immaculate, and much of the products on your order of business can wait until tomorrow and even until the following weeks or months. For jobs that require your complete focus, attempt not to multitask. Plan to place your partner in cost if you require to pay expenses or utilize the computer when your kids are around.

Harmony through the Structure of Family Members Harmony and Values Household consistency is a vital component to a strong household organization. Placement in vision and worth and strong dedication from family members assists business leaders to make hard choices that will steer the firm in suitable instructions. Family member's consistency and competitive advantage can result from this placement.

It suggests constant work and continuous reflection on actions that maintain a healthy connection with the family as a bigger device. Family member's harmony does not mean there are no debates. As Randel Carlock and likewise, John Ward state in their publication 'When Family Services Are Actually Finest: The Identical Planning Process for Family Members Tranquility and Business Success': "Organization communications are specialist in addition to temporal, suggesting that strategies call for premium and a sensibly short opportunity framework; household collaborations, in contrast, are actually psychological in addition to last permanently."

Structuring Market values

Member of the family tranquility can be helped by concentrating on an easy platform to identify and demonstrate the loved ones, truly worth and utilizing those as guideposts in relative and company dream, strategy, financial investment, and control.

The 5 activities of the identical planning treatment renting from When Household Services Are Actually

Utmost: The Matching Preparing Refine for Family members Tranquility and likewise Service Effectiveness.

It takes real nerve and perseverance to view to it future family choices and activities are based upon market values. Similarly, a vacant company worth may cultivate negative and disheartened team members. Thus, as well as we can easily remove family members really worth developing adversely and meaning participants of the household.

Patrick Lencioni suggests in "Make Your Values Mean Something" that services require to identify their core worth. He suggests that there are four different types of worth: core worth, aspirational values, permission-to- play worth, and unexpected values. Lencioni asserts that firms that recognize, adhere to, and cultivate to their core worth achieve a unique competitive advantage; so, also, can a family. When service-owning households stick and cultivate their core values, they provide the firm and their household a benefit in thriving over the generations ahead.

Values in Action

As specialists to the family companies, we typically start our collaboration with families by helping them identify their core values in action terms. Many times, when we ask about their worth, we get answers like "respect, stability, sincerity." Occasionally families recognize these values, however, then don't obey them on an everyday basis. One family had actually spent significant time on a worth work out thinking of the complying with list:

- Honesty.
- Integrity.
- Caring.
- Supportive.
- Togetherness.
- Generosity.
- Respect.

The family members absolutely counted on these worth but their everyday experiences with each other remained in conflict with this vision. This household's sibling group was brought down in competition, hurt sensations, and skepticism. In-laws were perceived as out-laws and the moms and dads had placed themselves as mediators and interaction channels for their children. At one factor, the brother or sisters hadn't talked to each other in fairly some time. Many of the worth they had listed were aspirational worth.

The worth of "caring, helpful, togetherness, and regard" simply were not their worth in action. It was what they desired their worth to be - what they aspired their worth to be - yet it had not been sustained by their habits. The group did not have sufficient trust funds built up in between them to establish the tenacity needed to achieve their aspirational values.

Attaining Actionable Values.

We hung around sharpening their list of values and breaking them into three of the 4 parts defined by Lencioni: core, aspirational and permission-to-play. Core worth contained honesty and kindness. The values of honesty and respect were identified as permission-to-play values - simply those worth that were considered essential in each people as a human being to come from a team. The aspirational values were identified and refined to function towards a usual goal for the family.

At each meeting, the worth was assessed and each person was asked to reflect on how they did or didn't live those values given that we had last fulfilled. Each family member did a great deal of soul-searching, reparation, and subtle altering to assist the bigger family work through their challenges. By calling the

actions and the value connected with that worth, the household had the ability to recognize how they can change their activities to start living the worth they deemed essential.

Several households have an expectation that their household has particular worth, yet the mismatch in between activities and values leads to frustration, ill will certainly, and difficult sensations.

Ultimately, the family stated right here reached "caring and supportive" as core worth in their activities. Through guts and persistence, the family was able to determine, clarify and eventually live their core worth. As a result, a few of their various other aspirational values relied on the core. Today, the resulting harmony in their family members has actually offered their service a competitive advantage over others in their market because of the adherence, time, and guts offered to their core values.

Aligning Values for Future Generations.

Other family members who had gotten significant riches from their family business were worried about the future generation maturing. The first-generation moms and dads had developed a wide range and feared about the capacity for entitlement, department, and wasting among their kids and their family members. A few of the siblings were contributing to your business, and some were certainly not. Their moms and dads had actually done significant estate planning yet had actually not connected any details to their kids. Soon, the brother or sisters (and their family members) would receive several of the benefits of ownership as a result of the estate preparation.

Each person had to choose 10 worth (out of a supplied list of 50) that they believed recognized their household. When the entire group met once more, each subgroup identified their values and the family members. After that, they functioned to discover a common string amongst all the values offered.

The next step was to connect the worth with habits in the family. As with several households, the siblings couldn't be a lot more variety in their personalities. However, when it came to their values, they were extremely similar and aligned. Creating this understanding about the values of the 2nd generation produced a brilliant place for the future of the venture, and for the household.

As a family member expands via generations, it is even more essential to determine and clarify the family member's worth in order to preserve the harmony needed in a household venture. Enhancements to the household via marital relationships generate brand-new worth which can be beneficial to the nuclear family. However, it might pluck the core worth when identified by the initial enterprising family. Each generational team should evaluate the core values of the previous generation (together with the linked actions) to ensure the positioning of family worth to drive vision, governance, financial investment, and approach. This can be true for a running company, a structure, or perhaps a family member's workplace.

Values alignment aids to clarify why the family members need to stay with each other as shareholders and assists the business gain an advantage - due to family consistency.

Kindness

Every family member encounters a situation where the actions or inactiveness of a specific family member has an adverse impact on the remainder of the team. These issues are hard to resolve because family members are complex and fragile devices.

Due to the intricacy, individuals have to be delicate and caring when taking care of household concerns.

The family has to come together, talk about the concerns and develop a service that considers the needs of the member at the core of the problem and the requirements of the rest of the household. Otherwise, bad moves can cause the department of the family and years of emotional anger.

Phase 1: Group

Producing a team

Involve everyone who is suitable and qualified for providing aid. Sources on the table and leave out family members who have vested interest while doing so and outcome.

It is best to stay clear of adhering to individuals when developing a group:

- Ex-spouses.
- Estranged loved ones.
- People who are submersed in family

members' national politics.
- Aggressive personality types.
- People with individual programs.
- Commitments.

It is necessary to ensure commitments during the planning process.

These include:

- To prevent passing judgment on the individual in question.
- To be thoughtful during every action of the process.
- To stay clear of individual schedules.

Phase 2: Questions.

The group needs to address some vital questions prior to any preparation can occur.

These consist of:

- Why have we gathered?
- How is this concern affecting the group?
- Just how has this problem manifested itself?
- Why do people intend to see this concern challenged and solved?
- What are people's purposes?
- What are we wanting to attain by collaborating?

- What do you think about an effective end result?

It takes time and concession, but everyone needs to get in the procedure with the same objectives.

Phase 3: The Planning Sessions.

Three factors arise, when a plan is applied, consisting of a timeline, landmarks to gauge progress, and a normal stock of resources.

Having an individual accept the service and after that not being able to deliver on the assurances of support and sources, will lead to a loss of trust fund and fracturing of family unity.

Other issues to think about when developing a plan:

1. Location for meeting with the member of the family.
2. Individual dedications.
3. Communication between team participants.
4. Available Resources.

- Friends.
- Programs.
- Money.

Stage 4: The Agenda.

The Agenda will certainly guide the group

throughout their conference with the family member.

It includes:

- Statement of Love and Support.
- The purpose of the conference.
- Solutions.
- Plan of Action.
- Possibility of Failure.
- Agreement.

It is a methodical rundown of whatever that the group has actually gone over and set. Also, leave sufficient room on the program to make notes and make changes to agenda products throughout the conflict.

Phase 5: The conference.

Opening Declaration of Affection and additionally Assistance.

Begin the chat along with a declaration that demonstrates the team's commitment to helping the person in question.

The intention of the Meeting.

Request every person's participation and make it clear that everybody has a right to be heard without interruption. Also, remind every person of the importance of the conference and exactly how it remains in every person's best interest to act in a considerate and respectful way.

Solutions.

Review the agenda at the beginning of the conference and sum up the process, dispute, and effort that led everybody to this meeting.

List remedies and assess the recommended timelines for these services. Allow extended stops between points to allow for adverse and positive responses and dedicate to resolving them during the conference.

Adjusting Solutions.

Conversation and dispute will disclose brand-new information and the team has to adjust to any type of extreme revelations. However, the procedure from starting to end has to be democratic, to make sure that everyone complies with the choices made by the group.

Also, try to engage them so that, they can contribute with their very own sources, consisting of supportive close friends, clinical or job assistance.

Be Supportive without Surrendering.

Listen to any kind of aggression or negativeness on either side and do not allow the team to splinter. A loss of unity will certainly allow the relative to wonder about the group's commitment and the validity of their issues.

In durations of increased stress, the, even more, self-aware, revered, and mindful people in the group need to step forward to manage the circumstance.

Take breaks and collect yourself. Everyone

included will require to be guaranteed the function of the conference.

Negative Outcome.

Every family member and circumstance is special, so even the most effective intents and effort might finish in failing. In extreme cases, the group may determine to ostracize the person, usage clinical intervention, or take legal action.

Arrangement.

When the team has gotten to a consensus, a modified Master Agenda will work as a contract between everybody included.

Every person will commit him or herself to the contract and warranty. They will certainly do their component to meet the contract.

Handling household issues is no different from any other complicated trouble that an area could deal with. The group should draw and locate a typical ground on each other's stamina to find services. Inevitably, devoting themselves to a typical objective.

Consistency if life through Hygge

Do not be misled by the television commercials showing women rushing between their professions and personal lives. It obtains a lot more difficult for females to attain a balance in their expert and personal life. Because it calls for taking care of both these elements by adopting a meticulous strategy. This approach ensures that you maintain your power hurrying, consequently achieving a healthy mind and body and a pleased and satisfied self.

Here are some feasible methods for the women of material to adhere to while attempting to manage their occupation and life together.

Discover harmony in disharmony

Nobody stated that it was simple, even, nobody ever before claimed it would certainly be so hard. From 'The Scientist' by Coldplay, I learned for many years that living in harmony with disharmony can be unified. When we're nitpickers, like many individuals are, we try to harmonize with everything we have-- consistency in our inner circles like friends and family, tranquility in our service life, and in structure connections along with our colleagues. Finding out the balance in our psychological and additionally bodily wellness.

Finding consistency in our electronic life with Facebook and likewise LinkedIn. Finding harmony in our individual and additionally solution enhancement. Keeping up today along with disruptors and startups to establish our organizations. Our team seeks stability in all our experts have and do, plus all of the needs effort.

Our experts may use panicked if something is not harmonious and spend a lot of power to obtain everything back to equilibrium as if getting to the best level of consistency is even viable. Individuals naively believe this is what they require to be satisfied, well-respected, and have meaning in life. Life is not like this. We need to determine what's important if we want to make it through in this globe, control what we manage.

We need to begin by being comfortable along with being uncomfortable. When we get to that factor, something occurs-- that's when we're prone and open for adjustment; open up to receiving things that are different. When we accept this, we will certainly conserve so much power, gaining strength and vitality and making us better individuals. The thickness of looking for the best consistency will quickly be changed by the lightness of residing attuned to disharmony.

Take the Duality of compatibility in disharmony and you'll stay gladly and locate assurance.

The function is life and daily life is actually work

Our company does certainly not stop playing because of the reality that our experts' age, our team grow old due to the truth that we quit having fun. George Bernard Shaw

When I found out that there is no such thing as work-life stability-- 'the job is life and life is work', I had an aha-moment. This outlook at work-life balance supplies us the impact to stay outside of work and additionally cease residing our teamwork.

Job needs to be life, along with if it is actually certainly not after that our team possess a difficulty. Any Project is actually enjoyable with participation, delight is actually in a similar way as necessary as effort, results, and likewise intended. And in the Fourth Industrial Revolution, our experts talk to everyone to accomplish while they transform, however, whatever takes place, work must be a lifestyle. If work is not a lifestyle, customization, perform one thing differently. At the end of the day, you need to possess the selection.

Don't live someone else's life

Life is too short. It could not always be what we expect of it at every moment, yet time is the only life component that cannot be expanded by an application. Use your time on this earth carefully; every min counts. Live your life with your body and soul, with power and enthusiasm, and while doing so try to care for the earth as we only have one. Do not allow other people or society to establish what you need to do, how you need to live, and what you need to be. Constantly stay real to yourself, and do not compromise that for anyone. I enjoy people except what they do but also for that they are.

In his Stanford University beginning speech, Steve Jobs, CEO, and founder of Apple and Pixar advises us to seek our dreams and see the changes in life's troubles-- consisting of fatality itself. Do not copy various other leaders, don't replicate other businesses or the Ubers of this world, and don't replicate Silicon Valley. Instead, take the knowledge, give them your very own flavor and make them your very own.

Don't be a know-it-all, be a learn-it-all

Inquisitiveness is the engine of achievement. Sir Ken Robinson

Be a consistent student, and never stop learning. Beginning doing some reverse mentoring with the Millennials and Generation Z. Open your mind and be receptive to brand-new things. It's lifelong. It never finishes. Wonder. Digital seeing will certainly require to be a daily play. Don't be a know-it-all, try to be a learn-it-all.

'If you just do what you can do, you'll never ever be better than what you are'-- a fantastic quote, go outside of your convenience zone, expand and learn a brand-new ability.

Do it with passion

Enthusiasm is the thing that will certainly help you produce the greatest expression of your talent. Larry Smith

In my opinion, a job needs to be what makes you tick and gives expression to your passion. You need to purchase life and get a return on those investments, so do everything with interest and follow your heart whenever feasible. It is like horticulture: nature provides you back what you purchase. Aim for the mind and the heart will adhere to. Share your interest and you'll make others sparkle with you.

Tinting Snack: have fun with interest. I recall a

business occasion called Leaders in London where the substantial bulk of the 900 solid executive target market looked grey. With very couple of exceptions, they were wearing black or grey. Benjamin Zander came on phase with a cello and a piano. He spoke about a few concepts of life, the link between songs and business, and afterward moved on to play music with interest, showing how to make a distinction. He selected a sufferer that had bad luck to have a birthday celebration that day, ahead to the stage and stand on the table. Zander after that showed the team to sing 'Happy Birthday' from the heart, with passion, with energy.

Finally, he asked the birthday young boy just how he felt. The man responded, 'I was elevated, I seemed like I was flying.'

When you do anything with interest, with emotion, with energy, various other people feel it. It will make your organization and on your own a lot more resilient to change.

Enthusiasm equates to discovering, finding out equals knowledge, and expertise equates to regard. And this respect requires to be mutual to prosper

Locate your sparkle

My leading requirement when employing someone is not to consider their organization or academic background, however, to search for the glimmer in their eyes. The very same applies when fulfilling new individuals. In French, there is a gorgeous expression 'Les yeux qui pétillent', in English 'The fire in the eyes. To grow and to be delighted, we need to discover shimmer in the house and at the office. Absolutely nothing a lot more, nothing much less.

Find your function and you will certainly find your glimmer.

Life is not a rehearsal

There is no bad weather condition, just unacceptable garments. Benjamin Zander

Don't anticipate a large play at the end of your life as life is not a rehearsal. Many individuals whom I know, seem to have a dream that once quit working, they will certainly do all the things they ever before intended to do. They have their container listing all set for when they reach their sixties. Reside in the now, and for tomorrow. The trip is the true incentive. Be mindful of today. When individuals strike their sixties, they will probably have various other restraints or physical constraints, so don't wait. My generation will certainly be functioning until we're seventy, the future generation will be functioning up until they're eighty. Life is not a practice session. Seize the opportunity, take the minute, reside in the currently.

Track your time

Assessing your existing circumstance is means stepping stone to attain a balanced life. Keep a timetable or log of the things to do for the week, including job commitments and individual engagements. In this manner, you will have a suggestion about exactly how are committing or losing your time.

Establish your top priorities right

Invest time to consider what is most considerable for you, and create a listing of your top priorities at home and job. Assess your time monitoring by questioning on your own. What do I need to start with?

Set concentrated objectives

Consider your priority list and turn them into strong and possible goals. Set details time right into your routine for different activities same as you would certainly do for an appointment or a meeting.

Plan punctiliously

The essential to mastering profession and life is how you prepare for your job and then work your plan. Make use of a day planner whether electronic or paper, this is the medium with which you transform your goals into fact. Spend 10-15 mins at the start on a daily basis to plan your activities for the day ahead.

Draw boundaries

Impose sensible restrictions on what you must and should not do at work and in your home. Have a word or two with your associates, exceptional, companion, and household concerning these limits. You could not be comfortable functioning late on some days unless there is a situation or a concern. Additionally, established a specific time in your home when you'll not look at or captivate any kind of job-related emails or messages.

Wellness is riches

This needs to include at the top of your priority list. If you aren't psychologically, emotionally, and physically fit, after that it'll have an adverse effect on your career and life. Make certain to eat healthy meals (specifically the morning meal), work out a minimum of 3 times a week, and rest for a minimum of 7 hours at night. While you might think all these as irrelevant to consist of in your limited timetable. These tasks make certain a relief from career-related anxiety, surge your power level, raise your stamina, increase your psychological health and your body immune system, and discloses a better and a lot more specialized self. Also, make limited use of cigarettes, alcohol, or medications to relieve stress and anxiety.

Cherish your relationships and family

Your healthy and balanced connections with household, friends, and close ones are possibly the finest resource of internal peace and satisfaction. If your job or job is influencing your connections, both aspects will fall apart at some point.

Happy lives through better relations of the Hygge lifestyle

Harvard Study of adult growth, the lengthiest research study of grown-up life (seventy-five years!) that's ever been done, showed that excellent relationships maintain us happier and much healthier. Not cash, high achievement, or being famous.

The large lessons about connections with family members, good friends, area, and in the organization are:

1. Life is work
2. it's not about the number of pals we have or whether we're in a dedicated connection
3. Great relationships do not just secure our bodies, they shield our brains.

Our mobile phone could be our push-button control to digital life. However, it is face-to-face connections that specify our wellness-- relationships that we need to humanize, personalize and re-energize in all times, and never ever take it for given. Support, respect and establish excellent connections in all areas of your life.

Indulge in some 'me' time

Sure, your health, job, and connections have a position of concern in your life, but it is likewise vital to spare some time for your restoration. Indulge in certain pleasurable tasks often. Extra at least half an hour of "me time" on your own. It will have a substantial influence on your alternative wellbeing.

And gradually, you will surely reap the benefits of the relationship and career front too.

Keep your work in your work environment

Master a psychological button on and off in between job and house. Carrying out such tasks after your normal job hours refrains you from providing additional minutes at your place of work which might even get to up to a pair of hours.

Consider your alternatives and work smarter

Look for the options offered by the company you're functioning for when it comes to telecommuting, flex hours, a small job week, or part-time work. You might come through a system that allows you to operate even more proficiently while saving enough for valuable household time.

Managing time more successfully is a skill that everybody from the accounting professional to the CEO requires to master. Using the best combinations of the time-management system can eliminate anxiety and save you some hours in a day. You can make use of modern technology to come to be extra thorough with your time. By organizing job emails and messages, and shunning laziness.

When do not get frightened by believing that you need to make these significant adjustments all at. Even if you embrace just a handful of these techniques, they will have a helpful and significant impact on your life.

7
THE BASIC UNDERSTANDING TO HAPPINESS

If you had visited the Danish capital of Copenhagen once, then you might notice something a little different compared to other big cities. It might be just exciting and full of things to explore as any other but the people there don't seem stressed out or in a hurry. It's not a fast-paced city, but a slow one, and all that matters here, is to be happy by all means.

The Danes know how to find joy in life by maintaining their hygge, and Denmark is mostly ranked as one of the world's happiest countries. This could be down to hygge, the Danish concept that involves creating a warm and contented atmosphere, as well as being in the moment and enjoying the simple pleasures in life with loved ones.

The good news is that, as with the best things in

life, hygge is free and very cheap. As Meik Wiking points out in his book The Little Book of Hygge, "Hygge is about enjoying the simple pleasures in life and can be achieved on a shoestring budget."

Here are eight things the Danes do to bring a little more happiness into their lives and that you can too.

On your bike

If you ever visit Copenhagen again, you'll notice it isn't just a bike-friendly city, but it's a bike-dominated place. You'll see more bicycles than cars in the center, and the city is covered by 350km of cycle paths and lanes. How does cycling help up your hygge? It forces you to slow down and take in your surroundings. "You can see and sense people in a different way when you're on a bike," says Jeppe Linnet, an anthropologist who researches hygge.

Light up

The Danes buy more candles than those of any other nationals in Europe, and they're a key component in creating a warm, inviting, and hyggelit atmosphere. They're not just for winter, either. In summer tea lights in gardens and patios create a feeling of coziness, even when the nights are balmy. You don't need to bankrupt yourself on expensive scented versions all flames are equal when it comes to hygge.

Keeping the kettle on

Meik Wiking surveyed Danes to see what they most associate with Hygge. The top response was hot drinks, with 85% of people equating them with a feeling of hygge. That's why in Copenhagen you'll find countless cozy cafes to while away the hours with a cup of coffee, tea, or hot chocolate. Not that we Brits need telling this we already know the power of a brew to make things seem a little brighter.

Slow down

You should slow down your cooking, that is. The longer something takes to cook, the more hygge it is. That doesn't mean spending hours julienning vegetables and creating complicated glazes we're talking about taking your time, not tearing your hair out. A roast chicken, a pot of chili, some warming soup simple but delicious food is the key

Do good

Help others to increase your own personal happiness. In Copenhagen, you'll notice many initiatives to encourage sustainability. Whether it's organic restaurants, solar-powered boats, or organizations like 'Too Good To Go!' A Danish app that helps you find restaurants near you that have pledged to help combat food waste.

Get soft

A hygge home isn't just about how things look, but how they feel. Hygge encompasses a feeling of coziness and comfort, and you can help it along a bit by softening up your surroundings. Choose blankets, throws, and cushions in tactile fabrics that you can relax under.

Back to your nature

The more senses you can engage, the more you'll be in the present moment, and so the more hygellit an activity will be. Taking a walk and getting close to nature — with all the sights, sounds, and smells that come with it — is ideal. Especially if you reward yourself with a hot drink and slice of cake afterward.

Be here now

Be in the present, and not to what's happening on the internet. "It's not that electronic devices are totally banned from hygge but in many cases, it will mean putting them aside and being together for a while without them," says Linnet. So when it comes to spending time with your friends and family, agree to put the phones off or away for some hours.

The way of Danish

Have you ever felt sad and down such as during a photo session? These are some of the moments that have hit most of us and we are forced to fake a smile. However, no one else manages your emotions above you perform. And if you send out notifications to your body to smile, it will definitely experience much better.

When identified and additionally made use of in

the optimal means, it may lead you to a delighted and worldly lifestyle. As good thinking may aid to develop our joy.

Our concepts are actually a repercussion of our responses to various events that may take place in our life. It's how we answer the issues, that generate our mindset, consequently, our company needs to have to have a great way of thinking in life. It's our values that we live by or an objective.

Have you ever before listened to any individual state "I'm committing to living a splendidly irritated life, might I be unpleasant and sad for the remainder of my life?" No! It doesn't matter which family or social background you are from, the reality is individuals inevitably intend to have a satisfying life or define the life they enjoy living.

Once you understand that, happiness is an item of our own mind so if we intend to live a pleased life, we need to deal with our happiness on a daily basis.

Every day, we need to appraise the important things that make us delighted and enjoy them. Recognize them, and do even more of what makes you delighted and what does not to assign our energy and time accordingly. Why would we intend to do even more of what makes us dislike more makes us awkward?

And even if you don't know what makes you delighted, it is beneficial to uncover the important things that make us dissatisfied and seek to stay clear of those. This can be your primary step to creating a life packed with contentment and well-being.

Happiness is actually within our quiet being actually that our experts presently recognize what creates our company delighted. Our experts do certainly not additionally need to have to chase it or even take care of a teaser, go up a thousand stairs ... Contentment, actually, exists within ourselves starting with us and likewise ending with our team.

While a lot of people try to find pleasure using their riches, excellence, amount of money, and career and get surprised not achieving it although having a lean-to residence dismissing the Greater London Eye along with Houses of Assemblage, and bring in seven bodies per year. Joy and happiness is one thing that we pick for our own selves and likewise a technique we decide on to live our lifestyle depending on to our being actually.

For several years when I was younger, I failed to recognize the difference between long-lasting contentment and merely satisfaction. If our company chase happiness in product traits, our go-after for joy will never ever finish. Because our company stretches out to our own selves by gathering even more wealth. We tend to hope that our team feels the happiness circulation via our company.

In a culture where big companies want absolutely nothing more than make us feel our happiness depends on what they supply, the media pound us daily with commercials revealing individuals that more than happy with products that they offer, they have, stars, and their big autos, residences and smiles on their faces ... They are not keeping an eye out for you and your benefit, and merely want your cash, your loyalty, your dedication and create a world where the idea exists that their brand, their item. So, we possess it-- can make us happy permanently. Actually, when having the eyes wide open in seeking to be the very own designer of your joy, there is no shortcut to lasting contentment. Believe that we can go after joy with material things; there is absolutely nothing even more incorrect than that.

Creating and finding happiness through Hygge

There is a great deal you can do and every little helps to get to this ultimate objective that, everyone desires and you can start by producing excellent and happy behaviors. A few that I do which I would certainly be more than happy to share with you:

To discover how to start controlling your mind as opposed to being controlled by it, learn to practice meditation.

Nothing is a better way of understanding and letting go of your mind's unfavorable self-talk than discovering to sit there and allow the thoughts pass without suiting them and feeding them. It is about being comfortable resting with ourselves in stillness.

Social interaction is one of the vital parts to residing a satisfied lifestyle.

Pick a reason, a really good cause to hang out with them and support your time with them. You wish to avoid being actually bordered by electricity drawing creatures of the nights or even time-wasters.

Take in balanced and healthy and balanced. Our second brain is the intestine! There are actually tons of research study now legitimizing the value of looking after your gastrointestinal tract just as long as caring for your mind.

While you may detox your mind by performing reflection, you may detox your bowel by looking after what you eat and likewise in fact. I carry out an Ayurveda detoxification every six months to clean up any unwanted components away from your body.

As truly feel lightweight like a plume after that. It certainly not only detox your body having said that also your thoughts. Great carry out impacts our mood and it is actually quite necessary to recognize which type of food items perk one and which do not.

Our team is distinct in the methods we see traits and the ways our team assimilates factors. Since the latest superfood is chickpeas doesn't imply it will definitely be a superfood for you, simply.

Sometimes it's nice to wake up and live into the day and enjoy what life's virtues are. If we want to achieve something, or if we want to be someone, without a goal, the right steps cannot be achieved.

These are the things I live by to recover my sparkle to really feel content and well! Joy is all about residing in placement with your values, understanding your worth, and living a healthy and balanced, and well-balanced life.

WHY YOU SHOULD NOT LIVE A LIFE OF RUSH AND CONTINUOUS SETS OF ANXIOUS – UNHAPPY LIFESTYLE

"We are frequently preparing yourself to reside yet never ever before residing."
-- Ralph Waldo Emerson

"one factor specifies in these contemporary opportunities of ours. Rushing. Our company rushes to perform everything coming from obtaining relevant information to consuming, to creating a judgement, to additionally adulting."

Nobody even wants to be a youngster any longer.

What hurrying does is, adding stress, anxiety, and anxiousness to your life. With time, this can make a huge difference in your default mindset.

When we're rushing, we are staying in a state of resistance. Hurrying creates a state of awareness that transpires when we're feeling distressed. It's a lack of desire to be in the present moment, says

Sura.

Have you ever noticed how rushing suggests a sensation of lack? It is never simple to wait for excellent points?

Yet what's the entire factor of hurrying? Because we can hardly wait, we hurry to take the opportunity for all points, terrific hurry brings in fantastic refuse". Benjamin Franklin

Our experts hurry to wind up being an adult before discovering to wind up being actually a youngster. We hurry to have sex prior to our team know what sexual activity is actually all about.

We hurry to own a partnership before discovering more about our partner. We hurry to want to build a billion-Dollar Company before we begin working on our startup.

"Rushing into action, you fall short. Trying to realize things, you lose them. Requiring a task to completion, you wreck what was practically ripe."-- Laozi

Isn't that the reality of life though? Continuously relocating. We are always trying to find the next best point. We don't such as to be stationary. Whether it's expertly, directly, or in our partnerships. There is a consistent sensation of never being good enough.

When you quit rushing and slow down, you appreciate life extra. Things are more fascinating.

Existence requires energy and a goal. Rushing

permits you to survive the surface area rather than going deep.

The fact is that at every factor in our life, the only point we need is the appropriate nutrients to expand.

Life is a Process

Life is a procedure. Time and time once again as human beings we don't such as to comply with procedures.

Ralph Ransom once claimed that "life is a collection of steps. Points are done gradually. Once in a while, there is a large action, yet a lot of the time we are taking a little, relatively unimportant step on the stairs of life."

The feeling of rushing stops you from experiencing fun points in life. Since you feel they will reduce you down, and when you reduce, you really feel guilty and left behind.

Is a publication better if you can read it quite fast, or if you take your time and obtain shed in it? Is your work much better if you're attempting to do 10 things at a time, or if you put on your own into one essential job?

Is food better if you stuff it down your throat, or if you savor every bite and value the flavor? Is it actually a keep track of a lot better if you glance at it, or even if you put in the time to pay attention?

If you have actually a rushed appointment disrupted by your e-mails and text message notifications, is your time invested along with a friend or enjoyed one far better? Or if you can kick back, in addition, to concentrate on the person?" Don't remain in such a thrill to reach an objective, that you reach the goal prior to you are ready. Often, we find out such important lessons along the way. Sometimes, we learn more regarding ourselves and uncover that we desire something different. Place your heart into what you do, yet do not rush. Good things take some time."-- Akiroq Brost

It Never Ends

Exists an end to everything? I do not recognize, because there is never ever an end to the whole procedure.

We assume there is a timeline affixed to our life which consists of events like understanding our art, development skills, self-improvement, actualization, and improving our partnerships. In truth, there is actually no timetable.

Simply know to reside in today, as opposed to thinking a lot about the past or the future. Fully enjoy your food items when you eat.

It feels like our experts are the men in the computer game Temple Operate and additionally Train Surfers who are constantly posting likely to no end. While operating, they come to collect prizes to control obstacles in the process. Still, the operation certainly never ends.

That is actually due to the fact that the process

never ends-- there is merely constant remodeling. And remodeling simply develops when you are knowing regularly.

I suppose they would have quit showing up if there was an end.

Effectiveness

"As the years occur, a sense of deep-seated determination comes one; one seems to be to understand the advantage of brilliance and the risk of rushing celebrations". Carolyn Heilbrun

Take a mango tree. When planted as a seed, it is actually little and it takes years for it to sprout. It is actually accumulating the ideal nutrients while undertaking photosynthesis to grow.

And additionally what happens when its own sources grow strong in the ground? It develops fruits, for that reason it keeps for life till it disappears. It is actually a slow-going process, however, it's meeting.

The slower you go, the fewer errors you create. The faster you go, the easier it is to acquire prevented when traits decrease you down. Our life, job, job, abilities, art, connections all end as incomplete tasks. This is why one should continually strive for mastery.

Steve Jobs died as an unfinished job both in his work and life. Michael Jackson, among the best artists of all time, passed away as an unfinished job both in his job and life. The wonderful Leonardo da

Vinci passed away as an incomplete job both in his job and life. And yet, they are all masters in their particular area.

Three masters who achieved it all and yet still died as an unfinished project informs you all that requires to be stated.

Our life is a procedure. Our ability is a process. Our relationship is a procedure. Our craft is a process. Our service is a process. Our art is a procedure.

Knowing is a process.

Know this and you will certainly recognize that at every point where you are, all you need is the best nutrient to expand. Quickly enough, you will certainly start to grow as you reach your mastery stage.

"Never remain in a rush; do every little thing quietly and in a calm spirit. Do not shed your inner peace for anything whatsoever, even if your universe seems distressed."-- St Francis de Sales

Life is much better when unrushed. And offered the fleeting nature of this life, why waste even a minute by hurrying via it?

9
INCREASING OPPORTUNITIES AND ENERGY AT YOUR OWN PACE AND TIME

Do you typically experience scorched out with excessive of the job? As time passes, do you feel like you have more works in your hands to do than you have time to carry out? Or, you could possess effectively use your opportunity to complete all the offered projects?

The method is to organize your projects and utilize your opportunities properly to get additional aspects performed daily. It can easily help you to reduce anxiety and anxiousness amount and likewise come back to the office.

Time management is actually a potential that demands time to build and is various for each and every person. You simply require to locate what works most ideal for you.

Right here are 10 manners in which you can

make use of to improve time monitoring skills and raise productivity:

1. Delegate Tasks

It prevails for all of us to take even more jobs than our desired potential. This can typically lead to stress and exhaustion.

Delegation is not escaping from your obligations, yet is an important feature of administration. The art of passing on work to your staff as per their skills and capacities and get even more accomplished

2. Focus on Work

Before the beginning of the day, create a checklist of jobs that requires your immediate focus. Inconsequential jobs can take in a lot of your valuable time. Some immediate jobs were to be finished on that particular day only while various other useless jobs could be carried forward to the following day.

Basically, prioritize your vital tasks to concentrate on those that are more important.

3. Arrange Tasks

Carry an organizer or notebook with you and listing all the jobs that involve your mind.

Make a straightforward 'To Do' listing before the beginning of the day, prioritize the jobs and concentrate on the fundamentals. Make sure that these jobs are achievable as well.

To improve your time management abilities, you

may think of making three key listings: work, residence, and individual.

4. Set up Deadlines

Set a reasonable target date and stick to it when you have a task at hand.

Try to establish a deadline couple of days before the job so that you can complete all those jobs that might obstruct. Obstacle yourself and fulfill the deadline; benefit on your own for fulfilling a tough challenge.

5. Overcome Procrastination

Procrastination is one of the things that terribly impact performance. It can cause throwing away crucial time and energy. Maybe a significant problem in both your occupation and your personal life.

Avoid procrastination at all expenses.

6. Deal with Stress Wisely

When we accept an extra job than our capability, stress usually occurs. The outcome is that our body begins feeling worn out which can influence our performance.

7. Refrain from Multitasking

Most of us really feel that multitasking is an efficient way of obtaining factors done. But, the truth is that our company come back when our team focus and likewise concentrate on one point. Multitasking interferes with productivity and must be avoided to enhance time administration strategies.

Utilize 'to-do lists' and deadlines to assist you to remain concentrate! By doing this you can do much better at what you're doing.

8. Beginning Early

A lot of successful individuals have one thing in common-- they begin their day early as it provides time to rest, think and prepare for their day. Right here's the reason: This is Why Productive People Always Wake up So Early

When you stand up early, you are much more tranquil, imaginative, and clear-headed. As the day progresses, your energy degrees begin going down which influences your efficiency and you may not execute.

To quit dragging from bed and start waking up vigorously.

9. Take Regular Breaks

Whenever you find yourself feeling tired and stressed, pause for 10 to 15 mins. Way too much anxiety can take a toll on your body and impact your efficiency.

And even better, arrange your break times. It aids you to kick back and returns to collaborate with energy once more later.

Walk, pay attention to some music or do some quick stretches. The most effective concept is to take off from work and hang out with your family and friends.

10. Learn to Say 'No'

Politely nullify a job burden if you believe that you're already overloaded with work. Have a look at your 'to do' listing prior to consenting to tackle the additional tasks.

Now, that you've found out all these practical time administration suggestions, start by providing out everything you need to do, prioritize them, and determine what can entrust to others. Set up the tasks with deadlines set and arrange your break times too.

When you obtain clarity about what's on your plate, you'll be much more concentrated and get more done in much less time!

Great time administration needs a daily method of focusing on tasks and arranging them in such a way that, it gets spare opportunity while obtaining so much more. If they can help you, utilize the above strategies for a couple of weeks and see!

10

EFFECTS OF COLORS ON FEELINGS

Researchers have studied the effect of shade on our mood, health and wellness, and method of thinking for years. Our choice of one color over another might have something to do with the method shade makes us really feel.

Light is absorbed by the eye and exchanged with another form of energy, which allows us to see the shade. This energy influences and is felt even by people without sight. Light energy boosts the pineal and pituitary glands, which control hormonal agents and other physical systems in the body.

We understand that red boosts heat the body and delights, increases the heart price, brain wave activity, and respiration. Mothers are urged to stimulate infants' brains by dangling mobiles including bright red balls on them.

Hypertension or bad control afflict an individual, they should not embellish their areas with the shade red if high blood stress.

Pink has a comforting result and can also loosen up the muscles. Pink's tranquilizing result has obtained its entrance in jails, health center spaces, and medicine.

Are there particular eaters in your kitchen? Attempt making use of orange table linen or placemats. Orange promotes cravings and decreases fatigue. Of course, if you're on a diet plan, stay clear of oranges.

Yellow is a memory stimulator. A touch of yellow in every room might simply aid you to bear in mind where you left your keys or eyeglasses. Yellow likewise increases blood pressure and pulse rate but not according to red does.

Environment-friendly reminds us of spring and thus, new beginnings. It brings feelings of calmness, expectancy, and hope, and it has a comfortable, relaxing effect on the body in addition to the mind. Still on that diet? Eco-friendliness is excellent as it might aid control the anxiousness connected with the technique of controlling yourself from spontaneous and over-eating. Perhaps, that avocado green refrigerator isn't such a negative point besides.

Blue is another relaxing color. Pleasant fantasies could be the completion outcome of coloring the bedroom in tones of blue. It has a soothing impact on the body. It decreases high blood pressure, heart price and respiration and in warm, damp weather have a cooling result.

One more research study reveals that blue in the classroom can be a good idea. Youngsters susceptible to temper tantrums and hostile habits ended up being calmer after remaining in a class painted blue. Both blind and sighted children reacted the exact same when put in blue environments.

More probable than not, if a specific shade is preferred, it probably is required by the body. The positive and enticing response the body offers is a type of "thank you" from body to brain.

11

SELF-CARE AND SURVIVAL

You should be always there for others, but never leave yourself behind of your friends and others.

The healthy hygge

Various aspects of hygge are very healthy such as reducing stress, biking and hiking, home-cooked meals, and having time with friends. Stress management, physical activity, and healthy eating are all staples of a healthy, happy life. When those things also happen to bring you comfort, that's an added bonus. But hygge isn't always healthy.

Unhealthy hygge

It is not everything that brings a sense of comfort that is good for your health. It's hygge to go for a long walk with friends and family. But it's also hygge to sit around eating cake. Sweets and alcohol are strongly associated with hygge. So is curling up on the sofa and watching TV.

Unhealthy eating and sedentary lifestyles may bring comfort to some, they don't contribute to good health.

The best approach towards hygge is to focus on the healthy things that make you feel good and avoiding the unhealthy things that bring comfort. You may find both exercise and watching television hygge, but one of those activities is good for you while the other is not.

Save

Occasionally, when we're feeling really stressed and running around dealing with everybody else, the healthiest point we can do is to stop and take into consideration how we can care for ourselves only.

While is evident to most of some people, and several of us have had a hard time with the idea of expressing ourselves. We were elevated to believe that, we ought to constantly put others before ourselves and neglect our very own requirements-- that it is somehow egotistic or self-indulgent, and not a nice thing to do.

Why is self-care not held in high respect as the necessary method that it is for our well-being?

Below, I have taken a look at some mistaken beliefs that hold us back from looking after one of the most important people in our lives. I checked out why self-care is better for others around us, and shared my own list of self-care commitments, as somebody that has actually struggled with this in the past.

1. We assume that self-care means being egocentric.

Handling ourselves is the contrary of being actually self-seeking. Because it enhances us and allows us to support our loved ones much better. We are no use to any individual if our power is diminished since we have actually provided every last little it away. Self-care is an antidote to anxiety, as it constructs durability so we can better manage obstacles.

Simply believe exactly how they tell us to place on our oxygen mask initially on an aircraft before we assist others. Yes, absolutely sustain others, yet support on your own.

2. We do not differentiate between "rescuing" and caring.

Due to the fact that we're too active trying to conserve everybody else, we often compromise self-care. People have to discover their own lessons in life, nevertheless uncomfortable that is. What are you to make a decision that you recognize is right for them? Since it is egocentric, as it's based on your very own wishes for them, which might not really remain to their benefit.

The method we can assist is to focus on ourselves and stop attempting to run others' lives. While we believe we're caring by "rescuing" them from unpleasant experiences in their lives, we are denying the possibility to encounter their very own difficulties, and grow stronger or learn a lesson coming from doing so.

It has been actually a hard truth for me to deal with, as I constantly thought I was behaving and caring. It's even harder to accept since a close member of my family of mine is very ill, primarily caused by their own actions. I have an overwhelming desire to aid and have actually tried out many events. Yet I now realize that they need to wish to alter.

By saving them whenever, out of what we believe is love, the remainder of the family members are allowing him or her to remain helpless. And we are shedding ourselves out with stress. I don't suggest we never ought to assist individuals. But there is a distinction between providing support for someone that asks and taking it upon ourselves to conserve someone and make their life turn out in a manner that we believe it should.

3. We are accustomed to connections based on neediness, not real love.

We frequently love the idea of being in love, because we regard Hollywood movies that portray love as remarkable and required to be with somebody 24/7.

When we offer from this place, we provide

excessive, since our company believes we have to die for that person and various other such dramatic declarations. "The most unpleasant point is losing on your own in the process of caring somebody too much and failing to remember that you are special also."

Instead of investing our every waking hour thinking of that other individual and forgetting us, us (and our partners!) would certainly be better offered by concentrating on ourselves. By doing this, we'll be able to offer from a location of wholeness, without expecting anything in return or sensation resentful.

As Rollo May said, "Love is normally puzzled with dependence; but in point of fact, you can just enjoy symmetrical to your ability for freedom." If we take care of ourselves, we are much more independent, less clingy of obtaining focus or love, and more capable of really connecting with another human.

4. We do not recognize we teach people how to treat us.

We show people just how to treat us by our own activities and mindset toward ourselves. By placing indications out there that you are a rescuer and will certainly compromise on your own to assist others. You draw in the type of people who intend to be saved and for whom it has to be everything about them-- not a well-balanced connection.

You have actually made it a self-fulfilling revelation, through successfully producing what you regularly whine that you entice: folks that capitalize on your amiability.

Below, it works to examine whether they have actually definitely taken whatever our team possesses or even if we have actually willingly offered all of it to all of them. Yes, they have in fact had a place in, yet we cannot alter them. Our team simply possesses management over our quite personal actions. Therefore what component did our experts take part in?

Take a long hard look right now...

5. Our team expects others to deal with our company.

While our company might think that our tasks are solely non-selfish and caring, are our experts definitely expecting quid pro quo? I have formerly been guilty of giving whatever and thinking about how I was behaving. Yet after that, really feeling resentful when they certainly didn't give back in equivalent action.

I grumbled to my friends that this or that individual really did not provide me sufficient (and, in many cases, I would not have actually been wrong!). It's simple to whine about what others aren't doing. It's difficult to accept that we have picked to offer all our love to them and maintain none for ourselves, expecting them to load a space they couldn't fill up.

Since it was our very own self-esteem that was missing out on.

Yes, someone may make use of your caring nature. However, if you lie down to be walked on, you cannot be shocked when people treat you like a mat. Your self-care is your obligation, nobody else's.

6. We don't recognize our well worth.

Inevitably, it comes down to the truth that we believe others are worth greater than us. If we are positive in our love for ourselves and treat ourselves as if we merit, then that is what we will attract back.

Yes, I'm scared it boils down to that whole self-love thing once again! There is a reason this is an adage, though! Because the secret to purposeful partnerships definitely is actually to enjoy our own selves.

Thus, What Does Self-Care Look Like?

Self-care is important for all of us but looks different from one person to another. Occasionally, our experts cannot also hear our personal inner guide due to the fact that our company is thus hectic preparing for the needs of those our team love so that you could have listened properly.

Below is my very own individual checklist of self-care practices. I wish it offers you some motivation for ways to take care of yourself.

I commit to:

1. Being fully in and embracing today's moment-- conscious living.

2. Preparing and consuming 3 healthy meals a day, staying clear of sugar fixes.

3. Getting outside every day.

4. Working out daily.

5. Doing something I enjoy every day-- being creative.

6. Hanging out with positive people.

7. Establishing healthy and balanced boundaries-- saying 'no' regularly.

8. Recognizing unfavorable self-talk and transforming it to favorable.

9. Stopping before responding-- do I actually wish to do this?

10. Getting something done on a daily basis, and commemorating this success.

11. Looking after my health, body, skin, hair, teeth-- routine consultations.

12. Being grateful-- starting every day with at least 3 things I am appreciative for.

13. Regular yoga exercise and meditation.

14. Chuckling more and beginning the day with a smile.

15. Singing or dancing whenever possible.

16. Having more fun and taking life much less seriously.

17. Treating myself with love and concern-- being my very own best friend.

18. Focusing on myself and prioritizing my

requirements-- not concentrating on the lives of others.

19. Spending time alone and being still on a daily basis.

20. Being my genuine self, not what others desire me to be.

21. Paying attention to my internal voice/intuition and doing what really feels right for me.

22. Preventing over-analyzing a circumstance.

23. Limiting my time on Facebook.

24. Not worrying about what other individuals think of me.

25. Obtaining an excellent rest every night.

26. Enduring myself.

27. My self-development, no matter exactly how tough.

12
CONCLUSION

You are worthy of to be delighted. But in reading this post, you probably recognize that happiness does not hinge on the material assets we obtain. Instead, it can be discovered in the top quality of our connections with the people in our lives, with nature and our environment, and with ourselves.

Hygge may supply a description to why the Danish people are several of the happiest individuals on earth. One of the most crucial points to remember regarding this practice is that it can truly be anything you desire it to be.

The Danish principle of hygge translates to something like "coziness of the spirit." It's the sensation you get when you're snuggled up under a blanket with a liked one alcohol consumption chocolate by the fire. As a life philosophy, it's everything about allowing on your own guilt-free extravagances, especially when the world is dark and uninspiring.

"Hygge could be friends and families getting together for a dish, with the lighting dimmed, or maybe time spent on your very own reading an excellent publication," Susanne Nilsson, a speaker at Morley College in the UK, told the BBC in 2015. "It works finest when there's not also big an empty space around the person or people."

What makes you comfortable? What makes you comfy?

It may be resolving in by the fire along with a publication, or it could be a huge dinner around the table, giggling with your friends and family. Whatever enables you to produce a cozy environment and appreciate things that you locate to be excellent is the secret to hygge.

If you wish to see whether hygge living is an efficient means of enduring happiness in your life or not, the suggestions over will certainly help you get going

While hygge is not nearly ensuring you have these components in your area-- besides, the primary part of hygge is that you're feeling existing and investing quality time with yourself or your liked ones-- the book did offer up plenty of suggestions that assisted me to reach that feeling of coziness and contentment.

The tiny trick of Danish happiness

The key is in little things. And many-many such tiny things all around the city. In my mind, this is the true secret of creating joy.

It should come as not a surprise that the winter season is the most hygge time of year, and Christmas is one of the most hygge vacations of all. Embrace it by being with close friends and family, watching vacation flicks, setting up designs, and indulging in great food and drink. Go ice skating or sledding, and warm up with warm delicious chocolate by the fire. Sit by the window and see the snowfall outside.

Include hygge to your dictionary, and bring some joy right into your life with it!

FREE EXTRA CONTENT

MINIMALISM & HYGGE CHECKLIST

Visit bit.ly/mhcl1 or scan the QR-code and download for free the exclusive "Minimalism & Hygge Checklist"

DOWNLOAD THE AUDIO VERSION OF THIS BOOK FOR FREE

If you love listening to audiobooks on-the-go or would enjoy a narration as you read along, I Have a great news for you. You can download the audiobook version of "Minimalism & Hygge" for FREE (regularly $19.95) just by signing up for a FREE Audible trial! Scan the QR-code or visit bit.ly/audibfree

DISCLAIMER

This book is not intended as a substitute for the medical advice of physicians. The reader should regularly consult a physician in matters relating to his/her health and particularly with respect to any symptoms that may require diagnosis or medical attention.

Although the author and publisher have made every effort to ensure that the information in this book was correct at press time, the author and publisher do not assume and hereby disclaim any liability to any party for any loss, damage, or disruption caused by errors or omissions, whether such errors or omissions result from negligence, accident, or any other cause..

Live healthy through Hygge

-THE END-

Made in the USA
Middletown, DE
19 December 2021